The French Country Table

Pottery and Faience of Provence

For Netty

The French Country Table

Pottery and Faience of Provence

Text by Bernard Duplessy

Photographs by Camille Moirenc

Translated from the French by Laurel Hirsch

Harry N. Abrams, Inc., Publishers

Contents

Foreword

The cold kilns of Moustiers, Vallauris, Biot, and Cliousclat have been reignited and now, what is more, they are being copied far and wide. While the time for tin and plastic has come to an end, the myth of earthenware and ironware thrives. In the Provence of today, the "art of the table" has two sisters—pottery and faience. Both are alive and well, reminding us of those well-appointed kitchens of the past. Grandmothers reminisce and gourmands meet up once again to enjoy jugged rabbit stewing in a skillet, spelt soup cooking in Vallauris crockery, or a beef casserole simmering in its *daubière*. Without a food processor, without any electric appliance, we set off once again with a mortar and pestle to whip up an *anchoïade* or an *aïoli*. The world of collectibles rediscovered, we are brought back to a time of fine taste, especially where pottery and faience are concerned, to the charms of a table elegantly adorned with ceremonial platters. We have learned that eating must always be a feast—a pleasure that starts with the eyes and continues to satisfy all the senses. A humble salad served in some plastic bowl does not taste the same as one served in a glistening white faience bowl.

Potters and *faïenciers* have come from everywhere, creating everything from platters for modern ovens to slick contemporary lines or, conversely, objects by and large drawn from older styles and colors such as those of the *polichinelles*. Artisans are even producing those dishes called "consciences." It has all started over again. A true renaissance.

In the Beginning There Was Clay

The infinite shapes and variations, continually refined and renewed, responded to both need and imagination. Often potbellied, sometimes bizarre, they were always beautiful, soothing in their bulk, steeped in their origins, and covered in glazes. What's the source of this strange compulsion to buy this large wedding platter, or that cheese strainer, or that *tian*? Suddenly, mysterious echoes reach us and tell their tales.

Chance and Necessity

The origin of the first pot remains a mystery. How, during prehistoric times, did it come to be made? And why? The answer is quite obvious—humans are greedy beings. Never happy with a dismal pittance, we want eating to be a joy, a pleasure, a feast—not a mere necessity. The need to feed oneself, no different from any other animal, is quickly supplanted by a quest for new tastes. Humans were not only harvesters of grains, fruits, herbs, and vegetables, but also had meat at their disposal—both large and small game. Some four hundred thousand

The earth; the clay extracted from it; fire; the efforts of man to transform material into object.

Then, perhaps in Terra Amata or elsewhere, next to a fire, some man left his mark—the flames had hardened the goatskin and one of our ancestors had noticed. Thus, the first pot was born. At this point, all that was needed was to get some clay, shape it, and then bake it in the embers. The first potter of humankind had to make something that resembled a kind of bowl. Relentless trial and error produced pots, some odder than the previous.

The Kitchen Is Born in Salernes

. . . or not too far away. But no one can say how the first pot, or one of the first, was fabricated in the Fontbre-

years ago, perhaps even more, domestication was invented and fire was harnessed. In Nice, not far from the pleasure port, in the remains of a camp of nomadic hunters at Terra Amata, traces of this heritage can be found. No question, they liked their barbecues! But there was no pottery, no possibility to prepare a stew, no chance of refined cooking. Creative cuisine was unheard of. A goatskin, however, would be suspended from a tripod made of branches and filled with meat and wild vegetables or fruit. To heat it, some bits of quartzite that had been heated in the fire were added. The contents would come to a boil without damaging the skin. The result: a delicious soup.

goua cave near Salernes. Shaped like a ball or melon, it was about six inches (16 centimeters) tall and had an opening that was also six inches (16 centimeters) in diameter—a small pot for three to four portions. Scholars believe that the small ripples decorating the pot were made with a "cardium" seashell, or a cockle, which is still a favorite among gastronomes. Almost all that goes into pottery making was already present in this piece that dates back almost seven thousand years. Clay was already being combined with sand to prevent the pottery from cracking, modeling was done without a wheel, and decoration and glazing

Soft and malleable, the slate is easily extracted and worked.

were worked with a small, smooth stone. After drying, the pot was baked beneath a fire. Three kinds of pierced handles have been discovered: for transporting, for grasping, and for pouring (without risking spillage). Pots were always fired far from the flames, which reduced the risk of cracking and produced an even heat, promising good results.

Undoubtedly, both the Neanderthal and the Paleolithic cuisines continued to exist, and without pots. On wooden spits they would roast leg of ibex and delicious

haunch of bear, aurochs, or deer. They would also braise partridge and hare between the burning stones and ash, and, as already mentioned, in goatskins. But as food stuck to the walls of the goatskin, it would give a taste to whatever was heated in it, save for milk. With this new way of cooking in pots, there was another choice.

Pottery proliferated and the first soups were prepared.

In Fontbregoua, using the pot, fragrant herbs such as thyme and crystals of saltpeter for salt could be added to the soup, along with crushed reindeer marrowbones and

fats to heighten flavor. White carrots and some thirty other root vegetables, ranging from rape of bellflower to parsnip, along with spelt and wild lentils, accompanied wild-boar meat or venison. In the Fontbregoua pot, a stew could be brought to a boil, the liquid then reduced at a simmer to achieve perfection. Civilization was on its way. Some say that the marrow of these stews came from human bones and the meat was from the arms and legs of prisoners of war, but this has no bearing on the culinary quality of the cooking pots found in Salernes.

Willow twigs were slid into the handles to lift the pot off the fire and prevent burning.

The Panpipe Pot

Provence, lying on the obsidian, tin, and amber routes, has always been host to multitudes. Traders and adventurers would arrive from the East, bringing with them the farming and breeding technologies of the Near East. In exchange for products and the right of passage, they would demonstrate various new methods.

The people of Provence learned quickly. Throughout the Verdon valley, along the limestone foothills of Étoile near Aix, and around the wetlands of the Berre caves and other archeological sites, great caches of pots have been discovered. Bowls, rimmed plates, and decorated tumblers have been recovered, proving that a highly elaborate method of serving, allowing for individual portions, already existed. And so did urns, shallow bowls, cups, and lids for the pots—thus enabling the refinement of braising and cooking. There were also urns for storing the harvest, grains, and dried fruits. Some of these were distinctive with their spherical potbellies and short cylindrical necks, marked, above all, with an elaborate system for hanging that comprised a series of clay cordons in a perforated pattern and that resembles a cartridge belt. Or, more poetically, a panpipe. Willow twigs were used to handle the pots, which could then be placed closer or farther from the fire or on the coals, as desired. With the help of a lid, one could make a rather tasty ibex stew or a jugged rabbit in blood sauce.

In short, three thousand years before the Christian era (give or take a few years) Chasséen pottery was at its height. Prehistorians love its subtleties. They speak of the Chasséen of the hills, and those of the plains, as well as of the Lagozians. One fact is clear: from the time that cockles or cardiums were used to decorate the pots (the shells giving their name to "cardial dishware"), the pottery became more varied. *Fusaïoles*, or baked earthenware rings used for weaving, have also been discovered. These served as counterweights that enabled the lamb's wool to spin freely around a spool. Wool could be spun and woven, and fashion would soon follow.

Pottery became more refined, and despite still being modeled without a wheel, the walls were thinner and smooth rings of clay were carefully executed. This is to say nothing of the refined geometric, ladderlike, checkerboard, gridlike, triangular, or sunburst decorations.

Cheese strainers had already appeared. Generally, it is believed that these were used to strain the first goat's- and sheep's-milk cheeses produced by our Chasséen herders, and this is likely true. But many wonder about

Basic, but already indispensable: the bowl, in which the first lightly simmered dishes were served.

their use for juicing fruits. The harvesting of tubers, roots, and herbs, just like fruits, was women's work. Once crushed, cranberries, blueberries, strawberries, raspberries, and wild grapes not only made for excellent beverages but, even if a little sour, were still healthy and good for both thirst and digestion.

Nevertheless, prehistoric Provençal pottery still retains some surprises that date from about two thousand years B.C. For example, there was the *campana*, a bell-shaped pot also called an inverted bell. Its entire surface was decorated and its bottom flat so it could stand erect and be displayed. Its use is thought to have been originally ceremonial. In time, the bottoms were rounded, adapting them for the coal and ash ovens and indicating a utilitarian use. From this point on, the elegant bell-shaped pottery with its S-curve and its stability served new functions. It was no longer merely used for the preparation, serving, and storing of food, but to this very day, pottery continues to be displayed in social settings. As always, fashion became democratic rather quickly, and so came the end of prehistory.

Île de Martigues, the Gallic cradle of Provençal pottery, addressed culinary needs.

The Gallic Cuisine of Martigues

It was during the last millennium before Christ that the protohistory of Provençal pottery began. People had begun to farm, breed cattle, and accumulate riches. Above all, the human population was growing. People had to protect themselves from the envious, and many fortified towns, known as oppidums, had sprung up. Easy to defend, they could be found on all the hillsides, as well as on the isle of Martigues. Through good fortune, the interiors of the kitchens have been left practically intact and evidence shows that the residents of this period had rather cluttered kitchens. The Gallic Martigues house consisted of a single room used primarily as a kitchen. It was small and well organized, and had large earthenware jars filled with grains, fruit, and dried legumes. There was room for about ten of these

jars, which were set on stools for protection and lined up along the walls. Near the door was a cooking burner and sometimes also a clay oven. In Martigues, however, the fire was often made outside in the street, thus protecting the house from smoke, as it had neither windows nor a flue. During the Iron Age, the people of Martigues would always use pots, which became progressively shorter and broader in shape. Also appearing on the scene were cups and all sorts of bowls, along with kraters, jugs, and other items used for serving an exotic brand-new product—wine.

These house-kitchens were also equipped with a millstone, a mortar and pestle, and a sharpener for blades. The people of Martigues ate gruel, soups, dairy products, and meats, so a few pots and stew pots would be sufficient. A clay stove enabled them to bake cakes (which were eaten instead of bread) and perhaps already at this point, vegetable gratins and fish cooked in shallow earthenware dishes as well. With chickpeas cooked at a hard boil on a burner and a mortar in hand, *panisse*, something like hummus, was not far off. Although their diet seems not to have changed too much since the time of the panpipe pot, some new pots allowed for more interesting cooking methods. Flat-bottomed shallow dishes used for baking fish were more practical than braising on the stones. Pots and casseroles each had a specific purpose—whether for gruel, soups, or stews—depending on the size of the opening and the height of the walls.

The latest development was the arrival of vessels for wine, even though there were no vineyards around Martigues or around the oppidums. At least, not yet.

Everything for Wine

Massalia, the Marseilles of antiquity, was born two thousand six hundred years ago. Legend has it that Protis, a Greek sailor of Phoenician origins was seeking a new home and set anchor in Lacydon, what is today the Vieux-Port of Marseilles, where he won the heart of Gyptis, the daughter of King Nann. It was from this sacred union that the Phoenician city would be born. A nice story, at any rate. Protis transported jars of oil, pot-bellied amphoræ filled with wine, and painted pottery in the holds of his ships. Knowing that he would not be able to take over by force, he chose commerce as his way to get a foothold. From the very start, no doubt when he disembarked, Protis presented the locals with Greek wine. It was a thundering success. The Gauls, which is to say the rulers and members of the nobility, who were the only ones who could afford it, greatly appreciated the wine.

So it was the Phoenicians, partly because of the wine, pottery, and oil they brought with them, who founded Massalia. Their motivation, rather than territorial expansion, was trade. The old tin and amber routes passing through Lacydon needed to be brought under control and new routes, along with trading posts and inns, had to be established in the direction of Gaul.

There were numerous Greek wines, such as Marsala and Falerne, that came from Greece proper, as well as others from Rhodes, Cnidus, and Delos. Very quickly, Massalia began to produce its own wine. Doctored, it had a smoky taste and was stored in goatskins or potbellied amphoræ that were thick with resin. This dense wine would be mixed with water in enormous kraters, the finest of which were bronze, while others were made of pottery. The wine was poured into a *œnochoe*, an elegant jug, and then into the guest's two-handled cup, no doubt so designed for easier drinking. Consumed à la grecque, even the wine of Massalia commanded a hefty price. It was said that one amphora of this wine, a measure of less than forty-two quarts (forty liters), was equivalent in value to a single slave. Moreover, proper wine serving required the triad: a krater, an *œnochoe*, and cups. Initially, this pottery was brought from Greece, but soon, just like the wine, more and more often it was produced locally, as the potters of Massalia imitated the work of the Greeks. Another import was coral, which the Gallic warriors liked to use for sharpening their swords. But amphoræ filled with wine and the accoutrements that went along with it were luxury items reserved for chiefs and noblemen. It was very chic to serve wine rather than beer at grand feasts.

With the arrival of the Romans, builders and drinkers, came new culinary pottery.

Because these Gallic gatherings required them, people bought perfume pots; funerary urns; *lycethes*, long-necked flasks adorned with elegant handles and used to hold cooking oil; and *aryballos*, almost spherical containers designed to hold oil for anointing the body, that was the height of refinement. Owning and displaying this pottery, along with drinking wine, was a way to distinguish oneself, just as was using the oil.

Nevertheless, Gallic pottery held its own up to the arrival of the Romans. People continued to use their ordinary crockery, made without a wheel, and which consisted mostly of pots for boiling, dishes for porridge, and bowls for everything else. On the other hand, in the Greek colonies and where people chose to imitate them, whether because of snobbery or taste, in addition to the wine vessels, one could find casseroles and even skillets for frying in oil. For dining, there were serving dishes, platters for fish, bowls for stews, as well as all sorts of other bowls. No longer would these people eat like barbarians.

Living Like a Roman

Answering a call from the people of Massalia, the Romans arrived in 125 B.C., more than glad to offer their services. They moved in quickly and established Aquæ Sextiæ, which would include Aix, Arles, Fréjus, and other cities. Although the region was yet to be called Provence, it had already been dubbed Provincia. The Romans, wont to organize and control, constructed roads and in no time circumstances were assessed. The oppidums were emptied out and destroyed, their populations moved to new villages that were designed in accordance with Roman fashion. When Caesar arrived, he saw nothing more than Massalia and in 49 B.C., with difficulty, conquered it. The *Pax Romana* was imposed and the Gauls, by choice or by the sword, became Gallo-Romans.

The Gallo-Romans adopted the culinary habits and dishes of their conquerors and masters. Provincia became a land of wine, oil, and wheat—cadastral plots, Roman farms, and flowering villas. It was in good taste to abandon the old pots, particularly the Gallic ones, except perhaps in a few out-of-the-way, indomitable, untamed villages.

All the same, the Gallo-Romans had a vast array of clay crockery. First, there were the wine amphoræ which, having achieved a certain "democratization," were widely used. Then there were the amphoræ for oil, brine, fish, and the transport of oysters. And even earthenware flasks for garum, an extremely salty sauce that was made from sea bass, primarily in Fréjus, and is similar to today's nuoc-mam sauce from Vietnam.

Culinary methods required the use of cups and mortars in which dough could be prepared for breads, biscuits, and cakes. These cups had round bellies and broad openings that made kneading easy. Cooking was done in a flat platter that had a rounded belly and rather high sides, and was known as an *olla*. This was the perfect vessel for boiling water and vegetables and cooking fruit or soups garnished with a little meat. The Gallo-Roman who wanted to cook fish or prepare a stew or a steamed dish would use a medium-deep covered casserole that stood on feet to avoid direct contact with the coals. A fundamental part of the Roman kitchen, the *patina* was used to simmer stews with a sauce base, a dish to which it would lend its name. As for the sauce pan, it resembled an *olla* but was shallower and could be used for boiling, browning, and simmering.

For their table service, they had plates or *patelles* (shallow dishes) with raised rims, but above all, they used bowls for serving portions of fish, chickpeas or leeks, chicken, biscuits, and so on. For drinking, small urns were used and two-handled amphoræ that held water were set on the table. Wine was first poured into a narrow-necked jug and then into some kind of mug (which could even have been a *patère* or shallow saucer), or a cup with a flared rim or, in the home of the wealthy, a chalice.

This earthenware was often made in true pottery factories, such as in Fréjus, of ordinary clay. Occasionally it came from Campanie or, more often, from southwest Gaul, and was red and stamped with decorations. Astonishingly, the Romanized Gauls of Provincia already ate from mass-produced dishes.

The Clay Is Gray

The *Pax Romana* lasted several centuries until the Romans gave way to the barbarians. Chaos, hopelessness, and fear took root and the pottery found from this time bears this out. Gone are the banquet platters, the amphoræ, the bowls and plates. And for hundreds of years, the people of Provence lost even the memory of them. There remained only scant pieces of pottery,

large flasks for liquids and some round-bottomed pots that did not even have a handle and could hold only enough food for a few people. And a meager meal at that. Thoughts of porridge and thick soup were joyless—it was enough to survive. Even the roaming game were threatened by the endless plundering. Pots now served for cooking, storage, and preservation of legumes, grains, and garlic. As they were convex, to stand them up you had to dig a hole in the earth. As they went directly into the embers, they were made of a resistant clay that was gray and drab. Some had spouts for liquids, but there was no longer any wine, just the milk of the few goats and sheep that were bred.

If, occasionally, an enameled shard appears in the finds, it is because during this period the people of Provence were subject to invasions by the Andalusians, who came from a civilized Spain and who would discard their used or chipped pottery.

Unfathomable contribution: amphoræ designed to store oil, wine, and salted mussels.

The uninspired Provençal pottery of this period, that lasted from the sixth century up to the tenth, is a testament to all their misfortunes—a retreat to the far side of prehistory, a picture of a lost people whose only purpose was instinctive survival.

The Age of the *Pégau*

Starting in the eleventh century, a very special pot came into general use: the *pégau*. It was full-bellied, rounded, had a flat bottom and a single handle. It sometimes had a pouring spout and was always gray. But above all, it held little and was designed to be used by only one person. It was neither a plate nor a bowl, but rather an individual receptacle that replaced the earlier four- to six-quart (four- to six-liter) pot. It represented the return to a certain way of life. It was not the pot of a downtrodden people who had to hide like hunted beasts; it was simply a pot for the poor.

Great numbers of *pégaus* have been recovered from tombs. Placed at the head and feet of the dead, the first

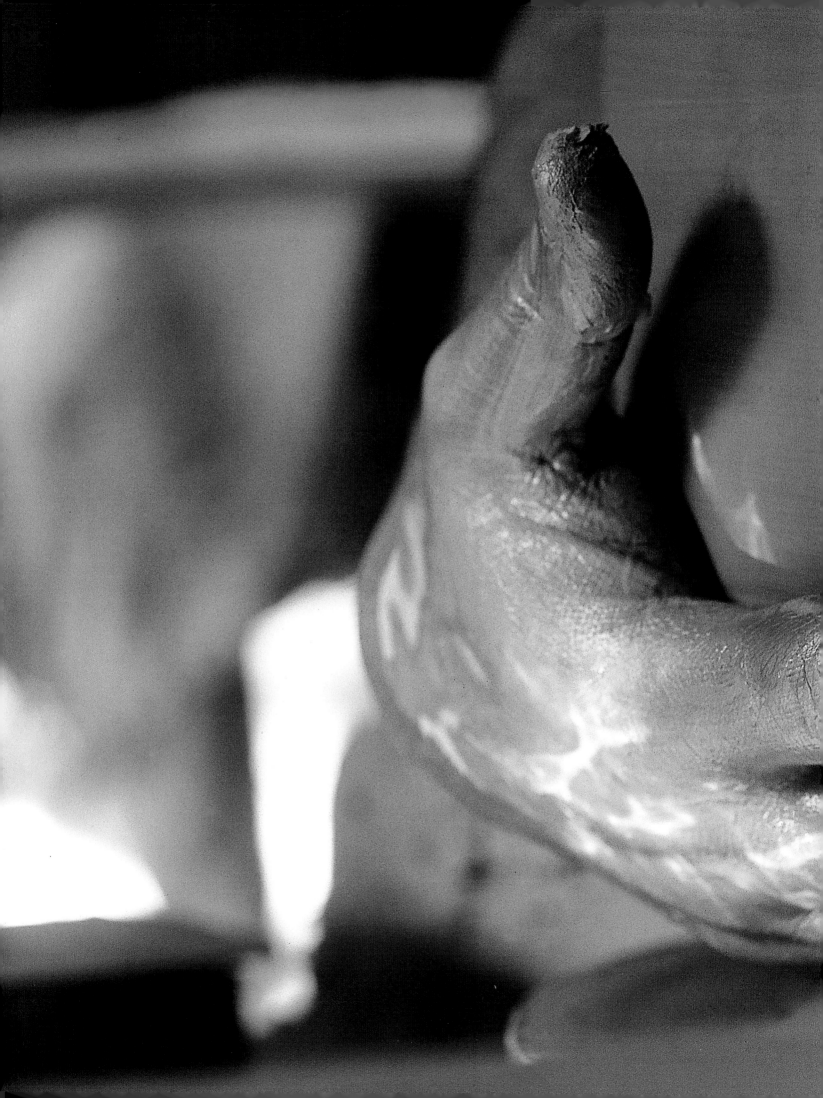

contained holy water; the second, incense. These were to ward off the devil, who was still deeply feared. Thus protected, the dead could confront the devil and then continue on to heaven. As people were poor, sometimes the *pégau* placed in the tomb was cracked or missing the handle, or it may have been the product of a misfiring. To hasten the burning of the incense in these imperfect *pégaus*, holes were pierced, facilitating the

combustion of the charcoal that was placed at the bottom at the time of burial. These funerary *pégaus*, reused after first having served as cooking or eating vessels, were the symbol of the rebirth of a better life, of improvement, of progress.

From the crude pégau, a poor person's pot, to the richly colored glazes from Italy and Spain.

The Color Revolution

The end of the eleventh century marked the beginning of the Crusades. The world of Europe regained power, feudalism took shape, rights were no longer only for the most powerful, the world was shaking itself up. And trade resumed. Ships navigated the Mediterranean, coming from the richer countries of Spain and Italy and sailing toward Provence. Certainly by the thirteenth century, the holds of the ships were filled with pottery that was to be sold. From the eleventh century, ships hailed from Genoa, Albisola, and Savona, along with Pisa and other Italian cities, and even from as far away as Paternò in Sicily and Valencia in Spain, all offering new merchandise: pots with a green glaze, platters, tureens, casseroles, yellow-colored dishes, bowls, jugs, plates, and more. Everything was adorned with rings, chevrons, waves, birds, or even arabesques—as some of the objects came from the Islamic world.

While in Marseilles the logic of trade took the lead, in Provence it was the feudal "manor-life" and peace that revived the trade routes and markets. Everyone, even in the villages, from peasants to monks, once again enjoyed the pleasures of fine dining. No longer was eating merely an act of survival, but tables were again decorated, if possible with a beautiful pitcher, perhaps adorned with peacock feathers, or a jug with a yellow, blue, and green geometric pattern.

Naturally, the richer the person, the more beautiful were the glazes. At the feasts of noblemen, pieces would be more refined or more flashy in accordance with the taste and the desire to flaunt oneself. But everyone, even the poor, bought at least some little piece of this new pottery, and so a market developed in response to demand. This style that had originally come from Savona and Pisa and Malaga would be reproduced locally.

Avignon, Capital of Luxury

The old gray pottery persevered throughout Provence in the kitchens and homes of the poor, but in Avignon, the city of the popes, power and strength were everywhere. Even on God, politics imposed its laws—to be triumphant one had to flaunt oneself, to shine. An old adage—"Put the small plates in the large ones"—was

invoked not only to honor and please, but also to make an impression, to prove one's status and, sometimes one's power. The popes of Avignon were big clients for the potters. Depending on whether it was used for a minced chicken with almonds and flavored with rose petals, or a simple *dariole* (a kind of custard tart), or a roast hare with a white wine sauce or some mulled wine, the dish would have to be individual in shape, decorations, and glazing. Tureens, which came from Valencia, were blue with flecks of gold and were decorated with thistles, holly leaves, or musical notes. This is to say nothing of the pitchers, the multilobed cups, and the jugs. But archeologists, ever vigilant and exacting, have verified that the clay used in the vast majority of these pots, in fact, came from Provence. The term

emerged because of the influence of the popes. The Lord works in mysterious ways.

The Invention of the *Taraille*

This was the Renaissance, and not merely for painters, sculptors, and architects, but for the potters of Provence as well. In fact, importation continued, but Spain was being eclipsed by Italy where geopolitics, the American Dream, and the dynamism of the cities were on the rise. The Genoese Riviera, Pisa, and Montelupe produced ever more beautiful pieces of pottery, including plates, pitchers, cups, vases that were almost

In Avignon, the city of the popes, pottery became luxurious, and the shapes, colors, and motifs more varied.

"Uzège" refers to pieces coming from the Provençal town of Uzès. By the fourteenth century, although there were still imports, Provence witnessed the birth of a local production. Whether it was the popes for their court and political affairs, the lords intent on luxury, or peasants who wanted to brighten up their lives, all had needs that local potters could address. The product was less glossy than the Italian or Spanish, with monochrome pots of white or green and simple motifs of crosses or key patterns. But new forms appeared, such as inkpots, flowerpots, and moneyboxes. The "ollier" quarter of Marseilles, which is where *oulles*, or casseroles, were made, became known throughout Provence. Already in place was a sort of fast mass production that

luxurious, and bowls, which could be found in the ports of Martigues, Marseilles, Antibes, and Toulon. The remains of the shipwrecked *Lomellina*, a Genoese ship that went down in 1615 during a storm, were discovered in the waters off Villefranche. Inside was found the marvelous pottery that the sailors had used. Platters for fish, basins, pitchers, cups and bowls with yellow or sometimes green glazing, as well as apothecary jars inspired by designs found in Damascus—all are evidence of the high quality of crockery used by ordinary crews.

Furthermore, Italian pottery did not arrive by itself—potters came along and set up shop. Beginning in 1423, a certain Pierre Olivari in Bédoin found

himself at the center of a scandalous affair. Aliot Forneri had maligned Olivari's mother, announcing to all that she had received men in her rooms in order to pay for the glaze for her son's pottery. The gendarmes were cited as witnesses. Aliot was condemned to pay a fine, but did not do so. He repeated his charges and gave Pierre Olivari a real beating. A friend of Forneri, another thief, attacked Olivari, hitting him with a stew pot. Our Pierre chose to leave town for Apt, where the affair was less well known. What resulted was the tranfer of a technician. Other such moves are noted, particularly in Avignon with the presence of Andreas Nico of Pisa in 1488 and Dominique Rebello, a potter from Savona who, in 1489, had Antoine Rebordini from Turin working for him. Nico moved on to Manosque, then worked in Aix and gave lessons—for a contracted six gold écus—to another Italian in Avignon. There was also Jean Angeli from Offida near Ancona, who settled near Marseilles where he produced stew pots, dishes, bowls, jars, chamber pots, and many other pieces. Not to mention Bruno Catani, originally from Piedmont and residing in Aubagne, who made various roofing and floor tiles, as well as pottery. The Catani family had been known in the field since 1424, which meant for almost one hundred years. Another potter from Savona, Petrus de Meriado, would settle in Manosque. These men hired their compatriots from Albilosa and set up workshops from Marseilles to Forcalquier, from Eyguières in the Alpilles Hills to Barjols at the gates of Verdon, where their influence prevailed. From the sixteenth century, there was a veritable empire capable of producing the most varied Italian-style pottery that was in fashion at the time, as well as *malons*, conduits for water, and the mysterious "*bistornes*."

Provençal potters such as Honoré André in Forcalquier and others in Cucuron, Saint-Zacharie, Aix, Saint-Maximin, Brignoles, the Huveaune Valley, Vallauris, and beyond, also worked in these factories. But all, or almost all, of the factories were based on the

Lightly decorated pots used for storage and, as needed, on ships.

Italian School, which had been learned through apprenticeship and imitation. By the beginning of the sixteenth century, the city of Vallauris had been repopulated by Italians. In Huveaune, original, unique forms such as bowls with ears, flat plates, and chamber pots were produced and decorated with tulips, anemones, and birds, their interpretations inspired by the style of Pisa. The influence remained Italian. Even seventeenth-century notaries, who sometimes were mere humble workers hired to take inventory at the time of inheritances and seizures, spoke of the "*pize* found in the kitchen," "white earthenware *pize*" and "blue-painted *pize*." Pize was a generic term (not dissimilar from America being used for the United States) and indicated the preeminence of Italy. Even the theoreticians who wrote books like the 1548 *Art of the Potter Cavalier Cyprian Piccolpasso, Master Vase-Maker of the Duchy of Urbino* were from Italy.

However, despite this preponderance, other workshops were established in Riez, Valensole, Castellane, around Marseilles, Aubagne, Vallauris, and Biot, complementing those of the Provençal Italians. There was great demand, the population was growing, and the art of living was evolving.

Potters, *Broquiers*, and *Olliers*

In the eighteenth century, workshops proliferated everywhere, but certain centers had only one or two artisans who pursued only one specialty. Such was the case in Cucuron, Lourmarin, and Ampus in the region of the Var. The terms they used were varied: *terraillier* indicated a potter who worked with clay (*terre*); *broquier*, one who made pitchers and jugs; *scudélier*, a maker of bowls; and *ollier*, a specialist in stew pots. There were also titles such as *gerlandin* for the people of Château-Arnoux who made *gerlos*, the word for jars in Provençal. A rich language developed to address all aspects of pottery making and spread throughout the region.

The circumstances of any given place were unique. Take, for example, the case of Marseilles, where bowls

Potters busy at work in one of the workshops that abounded throughout parts of Provence.

were manufactured; during the sixteenth century official registers state that some 100,000 were bought annually. Between 15 January and 15 May, 1543, 36,000 pieces of pottery were imported. Did this reflect the commerce of redistribution, or was it merely a glimpse into household life? The figures were all the more impressive since during this five-month period, only thirty-six jars came through the port—making it costly to smash someone in the face with a jug. Or perhaps this kitchen pottery was very fragile—but how was it replaced? Marseilles also produced roofing tiles, bricks, floor tiles, and *malons* that were sold in the Barbary Coast, as well as earthenware pipes. By the sixteenth century, on the other side of Provence, Biot and Vallauris (part of the earldom of Nice) had become well developed. These two villages are separated by only six miles (ten kilometers), but each has its own clay deposit—an absolute necessity if a place is to produce a pottery industry. Clay is specific to a source, and thus a unique production is possible. In Vallauris, the earth has two distinct qualities—it makes possible a pottery that is resistant to heat and that does not affect the flavor of the food. Add to this the talent of local potters to throw their pots in reverse, meaning they would make the bottom of a stew pot after having first shaped the sides and belly, thus reinforcing the solidity of the piece. They also produced tall, straight, and shallow stew pots, some called *gouttes* (or "drops"), rounds, *daubières*, pots with handles, soup pots, Vallauris skillets, "Swiss," "Parisian," and "Toulouse" pots, chestnut cookers, rounded and straight *toupins*, dishes, coffeepots, sardine pots, jars for grease, shallow basins, plates, brick clamps, plate warmers, lids for all their pots, pitchers, terrines, and pottery "to the centimeter." A full range that mimicked nineteenth-century industrial design. In time, they would also make toys that were small replicas of their pots.

They made everything from toupins *to pots,* daubières, *jars, and then, most certainly,* tians.

The specialty of Biot was the jug—used for storing oils, grains, dried fruits, wine, or water. These potters were also known for their soap-powder tubs and their *bugadiers* that were used for washing laundry with the fine ashes from braziers. Roof and household tiles were made in Vallauris. All these items were sold worldwide,

from the Antilles to Quebec, and trade prospered in the French colonies. Tourism and art would flourish in the twentieth century.

The clay of Fréjus, used since ancient times, did not have all the necessary qualities. The many potters produced a line of pottery that included bowls, tureens, cups, basins, vases, pitchers, and even chamber pots. But no pot for cooking. It was a poor-man's pottery that was sold in the hinterlands and was exported on tartans (small, single-masted Mediterranean ships), some of which succumbed to storms, whose cargoes are now, some two centuries later, in the hands of archeologists.

Around 1620, the region of Huveaune, with its small river that flows from Sainte-Baume and joins the sea at Marseilles, was invaded by potters. This might be explained by the water, the wood for the ovens, the earth, and perhaps also by the presence of the Italian potter Bruno Catani and his family. Catani was an enterprising soul. In 1656, there were some ten pottery workshops in Saint-Zacharie. The pottery was pretty, functional, highly colored, and decorated in a pleasant style with flowers or little scenes. The pieces were

Pottery from the countryside was gathered at ports to be shipped to foreign lands.

easy to use and the prices were reasonable, which no doubt contributed to the success of this pottery. As in Fréjus, the lesser quality of the clay made it possible only to produce tableware and pots for storage and transport, little toys, and the famous chamber pots or *bérenguières*, which were decorated with little flowers.

By the eighteenth century, Saint-Zacharie was home to about twenty workshops. Success brought exports that went as far as Senegal, the Antilles, and Canada, but at the same time, it stifled creativity. Potters repeated themselves and, eventually, passed the baton to Aubagne.

Marcel Pagnol's city, over which towers the Garlaban and which was populated by the writer's heroes, knew how to preserve its heritage—Pagnol, their clay *santon* figurines, and their pottery. Even today, the city breathes and its heart beats to the rhythm of the potters. This is nothing new. Since 1643, the presence and work of the potters was there to be seen. But the nineteenth century belonged to Aubagne. In 1825, that town was home to twenty workshops, then twenty-three in 1840, twenty-six in 1854, and forty by 1878. They produced everything for dining: soup tureens, fish utensils, baby bottles, pitchers, and colonial-style water

3   GOLFE JUAN. — Embarquement des Poteries de Vallauris. — LL.

jugs. There were also jars for preserving, and pots for salting, for jams, and for fats. But the clay was not heat resistant, so in response to demand, catalogues offered stew pots, skillets, and gratin platters that came from Vallauris and Saint-Quentin-la-Poteris in the Gard region. Clay was also imported so these items could be manufactured locally. The great success of Aubagne was the *tian*, which was a kind of basin. It is still referred to as the *tian d'Aubagne*. The imagination of the potters was vast and all sorts of specialties sprang up: water filters, flour pots for starving escargots, *fourmetos* or pans for the sugar loaves at the Marseilles sugar factories, urinals, cockroach traps.

Aubagne also produced pottery for horticultural purposes. For farmers, there were pots for seedlings, while gardeners had "Medici" jars. Production also included watering troughs for fowl, nests and coops for pigeons, as well as glazed funerary vases. There were even pots for strawberries and the *toutouros* or trumpets for the Saint-Jean festival. (More about these later.) Still to

Stew pots (marmites) and skillets by the dozens—by the hundreds—which were always glazed with care.

come were the Ravels, the Isnards and their *fèves*, or charms, for the special Twelfth Night cakes, the Gastine sisters, the Barrielles, Louis Sicard and his famous terra-cotta cicadas which were trademarked in 1910 and continue to delight tourists to this day.

This is to say nothing of the darning eggs, nor of the tiles, the architecture, and the allure of artistic endeavors that surfaced in Aubagne, Biot, Vallauris, Cliousclat in the Drôme region, and in all the pottery workshops throughout Provence during the nineteenth century. All of these will concern us here.

Working the Clay

Peasants work the soil and potters work it as clay. The clay they chose as their own must slowly submit to the repeated manipulations, the cleanings, the storage cellars, the modeling, and finally, the careful firing. Potters are the gods of clay who work the elements—earth, water, fire, and air—to create platters, stew pots, plates, and skillets.

From Extraction to the Wheel

Depending on the nature of the deposit, clay is treated either out in the open through a hole in the ground, as is done in Aubagne, or through a gallery or shaft. The work can be difficult and, if the clay is damp, even dangerous. During the eighteenth century, several deaths were recorded in Moustiers. Nowadays, excavation of clay serves several ends: from Saint-Henry to Marseilles, it is used for roofing tiles; in Salernes, for decorative tiles; in Apt, for faience; and in Aubagne, the Ravels have their own uses. Regardless, present-day clay is not treated where it is excavated, and thus the final product is fairly uniform. There is no longer any to be found in Moustiers, but this was not always the case.

Whatever its origins, clay must be cleansed of its impurities. First, it must be dried and ground into a powder that is then placed in a basin with an equivalent volume of water. A rake of sorts is

In the soft light of the crypt, the clay is worked, slowly and skillfully.

used to separate all the foreign bodies, which sink to the bottom. The water is eliminated using a sieve, and the remaining clay is transferred into another basin that is referred to in texts of the period as "the ditch for trampling the clay."

The resulting paste is spread out flat on the floor and a barefoot worker stomps on it, first trudging in concentric outward circles, and then back inward. At this

point, a cleansing substance is added to eliminate much of the oil, making the clay easier to work and better to fire. Occasionally, some ground heat-resistant terra-cotta is added, and the resulting *chamotte* is more heat resistant.

Slabs of clay were then developed. They could be worked immediately to produce very ordinary pottery. For better quality pottery and for roofing and floor tiles, the clay was left to "rot" for several months, a process that is extended for up to a year in manufacturing faience. The purpose is to improve the chemical reactions, ameliorating the plasticity and workability. In Moustiers, several different clays are mixed together to obtain a composite that adheres better to the enamel. Finally, the clay is beaten and allowed to "rot" a second time, allowing the air to escape. It must then be used quickly.

In the Hands of the Lord

The most ancient of techniques, dating back even to prehistoric times, is modeling. Roofing tiles, *malons*, interior tiles, some jars and ornamental pieces all relied on this method.

Then, during the sixth millennium B.C., in Assyria, the potter's wheel appeared. As it required considerable skill, use of the wheel spread slowly and hand modeling continued contemporaneously to the Middle Ages. This can partially be explained by the fact that some pottery, such as storage and cooking pots, was modeled by women who were of childbearing age and apprenticeship required several years. In Moustiers, a three-year

A final method entailed pouring liquefied or molten clay into a mold that left no more than a slight gap between the desired shape and the two walls. This was used in the eighteenth century, and continues to be used in Salernes for making bathroom sinks that they call *tians*.

Following several hours of drying, the piece is then worked on: a pouring spout might be fitted, the shape pinched, a design etched in, some buffing, the ears on a pitcher attached, or handles or other adornments added.

From *Estèques* to Mothers

The tools are simple. An *estèque*, a sort of arc made from sheet metal or wood, smooths the pottery with a

contract was established in which the parents paid the master for bestowing his secrets and methods. In return, the master was assured of food, housing, clothing, and care.

The wheel, with the speed of its rotation, increased the rate of production and the symmetry of the pieces. Calculating the amount of clay to be used according to the size of the final piece, the potter, with wet hands, would place the ball in the center of the wheel. He then hollowed it out and, with the placement of his fingers, shaped it.

The third method was molding, which used extremely porous plaster molds that absorbed water. These were often used to make *santon* figurines, clay pipes, as well as plates and serving dishes.

In the hands of an expert, simple, almost primitive tools smooth, chisel, hollow, decorate.

caress that rids it of all bumps inside and out. There is also a turner that has a similar function. The level plate serves to flatten the bottom of cooking vessels so that the heat is better distributed. And then there is the mother, which is merely a ruler used to regulate the height and diameter of a piece. Above all, there are the hands.

Porosity or Waterproofing

A choice must be made and it depends on the use of the pot. For water, porosity provides coolness, whereas pots used for preserving must be waterproof and airtight. The gray pots—the *pégaus*—achieved this by being saturated with carbon at the end of the firing. An advantage was that this coating also served as a base for the

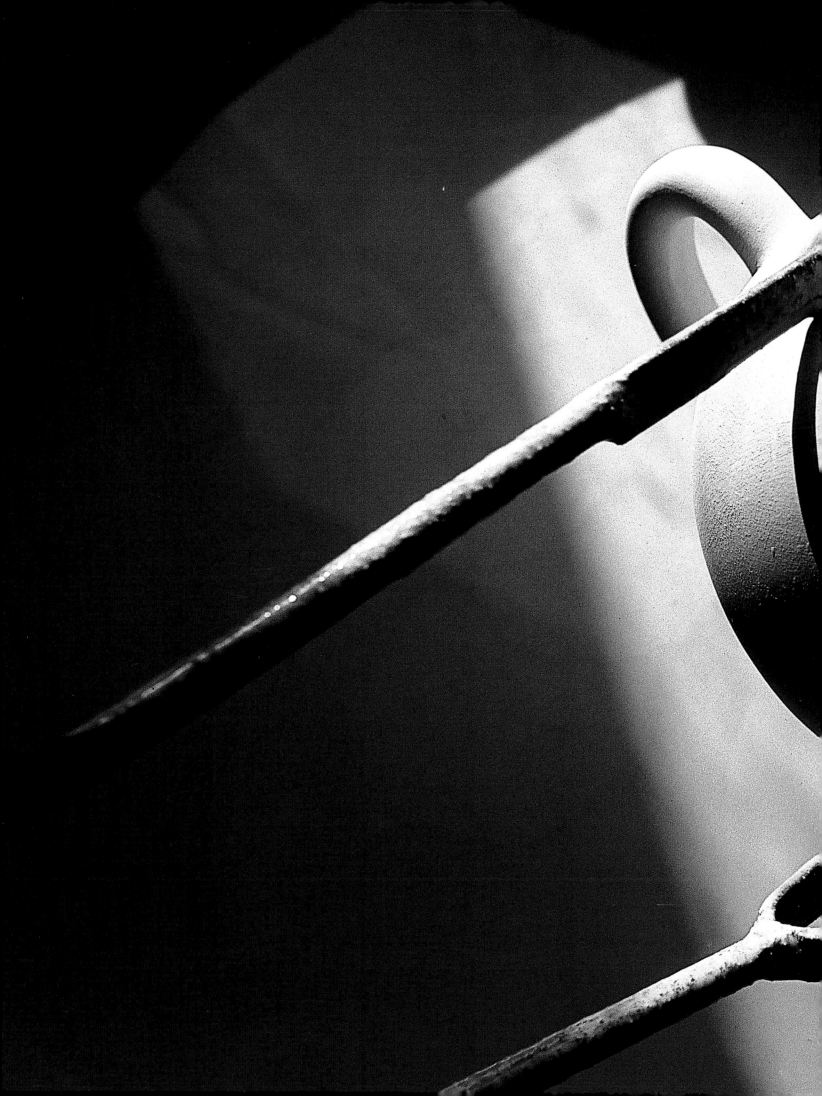

decorations. Alquifou or lead sulfide was broadly used as a lead glaze because of its transparency. For coloring, it could be mixed with various oxides, such as iron oxide for yellow and copper oxide for green.

For making faiences, a coat of an enamel made from a mixture of lead oxide and tin was applied after the first firing. The components were ground in a glazing mill and then mixed with water. The pottery would then be soaked in the mixture. The result was not only waterproof, but also had a shiny, smooth, velvety texture. The secrets of the trade.

Marbling and the Rest

Very early, through imitation, Provençal potters devised styles of decoration to entice all tastes.

One of the most spectacular methods entailed applying two coats of very fine, liquid clay, one white, the other red, onto a wet pot. This created a gentle wave-like blending of the two colors that was called marbling

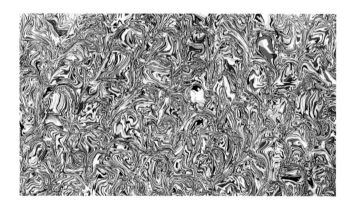

or swirling. But generally, the pottery was decorated using a brush or a pear-shaped instrument to create simple, often naive designs. Stencils were also used during the nineteenth century.

Mixed clays and colors of the sun make brilliant decorations.

Decorating the faience required talented, skilled painters. All the more so as the pigments would change color during the firing, the final result not being known until the end. Cobalt was used for blue, antimony for yellow, and manganese for violet. Painters, who used

the hair from a donkey's ear to make their brushes, had a great understanding of the qualities of both monochrome and polychrome.

The History of Kilns

In Provence they used a kiln with a direct flame. There was a hearth beneath an arched vault made of bricks, with passages for the flames to lick and bake the pots, setting alight any raw clay or tiles. The kilns were still small, but consumed great amounts of wood. In the nineteenth century, a kiln was developed with an inverted flame. The fire entered the baking chamber and exited toward the top of the vault and, seeking oxygen, followed the draw back toward the bottom. The firing now took less time, was more even, required less wood, and thus allowed for greater production.

Working in the kiln, where the flame sets the shape.

Between the firing, cooling, and retrieving of the objects, the process took many days.

With faience, the platters were put through a first firing that was measured not by degrees, but by the amount of wood burned. Then the decoration (a stannous enamel and painted designs) and a second firing, this time "at high temperature" of more than 1800°F (1000°C), causing the enamel to penetrate the clay. If the design work was done after this second firing, it was then fired "at low temperature."

The People of the Pottery

With an intelligence in their fingertips, potters have always served the needs of the peasants and sometimes even anticipated them. They are people who were somewhat tightfisted, obliged by their poverty to be inventive. They created pottery that could be adapted to all situations and products. Thrifty and shrewd, their pottery was beautiful to the eye, since life could always use some cheering. The first step always was to dream of the riches of the fields.

A *Grande Dame*— The Jar and Her Baby Jars

A venerable item that saw its start during ancient times, when it was called a *dolium*. There were enormous ones that were buried in the ground, as well as other smaller ones. But every *dolium* was a warehouse, an attic, a storehouse that was first used for oil. In Provence, wine would be stored in wooden barrels and oil in a jar. The clay gave off no taste and did not affect the oil. On the contrary, it provided perfect storage, clarifying the oil and causing it to lose the acridity of the olive.

tially, these products were potbellied and globelike, but then they took on the appearance of an egg, until eventually the jars were made round once again. In France they were called urns and had to be ordered several months in advance. Prices varied according to size. The base unit for measuring them was an eight-and-a-half-gallon (32 liter) cup. The client paid four-fifths of the total at the time of ordering and the remainder on delivery. The jar maker, however, remained responsible for his work up until its installation. The jar was not some trivial item, but a true investment that made up part of a mill's or farm's equipment. If it were extremely large— sometimes they could hold eighty gallons (300 liters)—

 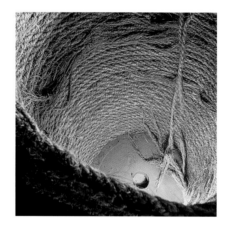 

When oil once again became popular, above all at the beginning of the seventeenth century, jars became more abundant. During the sixteenth and seventeenth centuries, those jars that already existed seem to have come from Spain, perhaps Valencia. Some of them were found at the bottom of the sea, filled with dishes and bowls as Jean Teysseric, the official corsair of Marseilles, stated in 1498: "*quatuor jarras plenas voyessela terra*" (four jars filled with clay dishes). The *jarra* was a protective mother before its arrival in Provence, even if sometimes it was used to transport musket balls. By the end of the Middle Ages, jars were being manufactured in Biot, which was their capital. The settlers who came and repopulated the Liguria region near Genoa, following the devastation of the black plague, introduced the production of jars. Ini-

The cord method— the inspired invention of a cabinetmaker turned potter.

it would have to be installed during the construction of the building, before the door was made.

Another problem was the making of these jars. Initially, they were placed on a stationary clay disk using rings stacked on one another. To eliminate any sinking, the drying time could run to several weeks. Around 1920, René Augé-Laribé, a cabinetmaker, arrived, and with his desire to become a potter revolutionized the manufacture of jars. He invented the corded wheel and mounting with a rope. An assemblage of planks set up like the sections of an orange formed the interior of the jar and a hemp cord was wound inside. Outside was a wooden form the same size as the desired walls.

The jar maker merely had to apply the clay, but this was no small task as the walls were three-quarters to one inch (two to three centimeters) thick, requiring almost two pounds (almost a kilo) of clay. Once dried, the inte-

rior scaffolding was removed by pulling the cord and the pot was then smoothed. The time for glazing had arrived—greens and pale or honeyed yellows—but they were not applied without the seal of Biot, which consisted of its four letters within a double-eight, first having been affixed. This is the souvenir of the sixteen families that repopulated the area in the fifteenth century.

Also found were the fleur-de-lis, a symbol of proliferation and prosperity; the cross, a sign of protection like the famous IHS, Jesus Hominum Salvator (Jesus Savior of Mankind); as well as the Seal of Solomon, beneficent message of his existence. No precaution was neglected for such a precious container. Once delivered and filled with oil, the jar was covered with a wooden lid to protect its contents, and was looked after by the mistress of the

house, the *bastidane*. It was she who made potions of Saint-John's-wort, whose healing red oil was precious and magical, along with many other things. The jar made its *Colombins would soon serve innumerable functions.* way north where it was placed in the cellar, if there was one; otherwise, it was kept next to the common room in a storeroom that had a narrow window, like a loophole, which let the cold in and preserved quality.

Jars were manufactured in Biot from 1810 to 1822 and 18,600 new jars were counted in the port of Antibes. It is believed that around 1830 production reached some 80,000 jars a year. Pierre Loti spoke of "a brig bound for the islands of the Levant filled with terra-cotta jars." They were not only shipped everywhere around the Mediterranean, from Spain to Turkey and Tunisia, but also to the Antilles and sub-Saharan Africa. It was even said that they were exported as far as Australia and to Paris, where they were sold at the Bazar des Denrées Provençales (Provençal Produce Bazaar) at 106, rue du Bac. For the most part, of course, the jars were sold throughout Provence. They were also ideal for storing water and the royal fleet of the eighteenth century was equipped with them, at least in the captain's service. Provençal kitchens all *Doliums, jars, and jarrons— a kind and generous family.* had several jars of different sizes that were largely used for water. Biot was not the only manufacturing center; smaller jars were made in Salernes, Aubagne, and Fréjus.

Along with storing water and oil, the jars were used for cracked olives or for those prepared with herbs and preserved in sugar, a quite useful addition for a simple and pleasant meal. They were also used for the storage of "aromatic plants for perfumeries and pharmacies," or fertilizers. The jars could also be used to preserve grain, peas, dried fruits, in particular almonds, especially if they were to be used in the preparation of *orgeat* (an almond-based beverage) and *callisons* (almond paste candies) from Aix. It was not a problem if a jar cracked. It would be repaired with metal staples and then used to store walnuts, hazelnuts, or beans.

Whether using the *colombin* method (which entailed a long roll of soft clay and did not employ a wheel), or a mold, or the system with a rope, the jar, *gerlo* or *jarlo* in Provençal, was always made in Biot or Aubagne with soft, velvety clays that were filled with light. The shapes evolved and today we no longer use these jars for storing oil or almonds, but place them in our gardens filled with flowers such as orange blossoms or geraniums. As the outer surface is enamel, a network of tiny cracks gradually forms, a natural consequence of the different rates of expansion of the clay and the glaze. For maintenance, the pots must be scrubbed with a damp scouring pad and then waxed and shined. To create an aesthetically pleasing effect, it is generally believed that the plant should be two to three times taller than the pot. If white traces form on raw terra-cotta, it will most

definitely be due to fertilizers. All that is needed is to wipe the pot with a 10 percent solution of hydrochloric acid. As far as moss is concerned, bleach would be sufficient. Pots should always be elevated on tiles so they are not directly on the ground. This will allow any over-watering to flow out and will protect the pot from frost, to say nothing of good mulching. Finally, when potting or repotting, it is best to put some gravel in the bottom for drainage. Accepted wisdom dictates that the gravel should reach about one-tenth the height of the pot. These precautions taken, the broad *gerlo* can be appreciated for a long time, its drips of glazing around the neck catching the light of the sun.

The "Conscience" or Demijohn with Six Handles

Or four. It had an ample belly that was partially or completely glazed and either two or three pairs of handles running up the sides just below a narrow neck, and through these handles a hemp cord could be laced. Yellow, honey-colored, green—the demijohn, or *bonbonne* was always magnificent. A vessel for transporting oil, wine, or vinegar, but primarily oil, it held about three to four quarts (three to four liters).

It was the cousin of the *gerlo* in the oil saga. They would be bought at mills or in the marketplace when all the jars on the farm were full and none remained in reserve. They were also hung by a cord from a donkey saddle.

On the raw terra-cotta, colored glazes flow and sometimes there is the stamp of the potter.

The first demijohns to be traced were exports. There was a beautifully marbled green, brown, and yellow one that came from a well in Martigues, believed to have been from seventeenth-century Huveaune. Another was recovered from the *Dorothea*, a Danish ship that went down in 1693 off of Villefranche following a stop in Marseilles. The pot was found among the dishes aboard. Both were contemporaneous with the onset of the oil and olive tree renaissance of Provence.

At that point, frost and wars had reduced this pot to a liturgical role or for frying during periods of fasting and no-meat Fridays, or for preparing an egg, some fava beans, or fish. It returned in the sixteenth century when olive trees were planted, restrictive taxes were eliminated, and other uses such as the renowned "right of salad" (defended by the archbishop of Arles) were reintroduced. There were still other vicissitudes, but in the end the olive tree carried the day—oil was needed for cooking and for soap. Containers were needed and jars, *détaillers* for transporting, *douires*, and six-handled demijohns addressed those needs. This highly reputed oil was even sold in 1810 at the Lebon shop in Paris.

The workshops at Huveaune and Aubagne and the potters of Salon and elsewhere made the demijohn, which was also called a *bourrache*, for the delivery of

this precious oil to the tables of the gourmands of the day. One was Ronsard, who liked roses in his garden and olive oil from Provence. But others included the writer-gastronome Grimod de la Reynière, King Louis-Philippe, and the simple peasant at home in his farmhouse. The success of the demijohn was such that it was imitated in Saintonge, on the Bay of Biscay, where it was called a *bouteille à passants* (passers-by's bottle) and used for vinegar. It is true that cruets for walnut oil were already in use.

Everyone used it according to his need. Thus in Arles, the *bonbonne* was called a "conscience" because after having taxed it, the archbishop asked for oil as alms for the poor. And everyone gave according to his soul and "conscience." In Saint-Chamas, north of the Berre marshes where the winter mistral winds blow fiercely, the oil would congeal in the jars. To liquefy it, a *bonbonne-douire-conscience* would be filled with boiling water and, after a string was attached, would be lowered into the jar.

The "conscience" or demijohn for the most mundane uses, with multiple handles.

The *bonbonne* is no longer in vogue. It has lost its beauty in overabundance—you can buy one, two, or even three "consciences."

Pots for Preserving

Provision faite en saison,
et gouvernée par la raison,
fait venir bonne la maison.

A venerable preserving pot that closes as tightly as a safe.

(Provisions done in season,
and then cared for with reason,
will make a house pleasing.)

A proverb that Olivier de Serres recited in his Théâtre d'Agriculture et Mesnage des Champs in 1599 under Henri IV, the king famous for his Sunday *poulet au pot* (potted chicken). In this period of peace and reconstruction, the preserving pot held forth.

Olivier recommended the use of jams, preserved olives, capers, quinces and other preserved fruits, peas, and fava beans in the pod, as well as *syrop rozat laxatif* (a rose petal syrup with laxative properties) made from crimson roses that had to be preserved in a glazed or "glassed" earthenware vase. He also stocked fats, using the fat encasing beef kidneys, pork fat, and the yellow chicken fat that was very desirable for soups. Salted meats, goat and mutton, fish and, in Nice, anchovies would find themselves in these preserving pots. And in Haute-Provence, butter, eggs, and also truffles in honey, fat, and oil were preserved.

It must be said that primarily it was dried peas, fruits, grains, onions, garlic, wine, and oil that would be preserved in large and small jars or out in the open air.

Preserving pots were used for products that were both less plentiful and more expensive by traditional classical standards, such as fats, salt, and sugar used to inhibit fermentation and rotting. Apparently the pots were also intended to be used for making jams and preserved fruits. In the sixteenth century, Nostradamus de Salon wrote a treatise "on the ways and manner of making all conserves whether in sugar, honey, or cooked wine." He recommended the use of an "earthenware terrine" and a "glazed terrine" for preserving the "rind and flesh of a lemon with sugar." He later referred to "glazed earthenware dishes." And similarly, for best preserving oranges and gourds, or for mulled wines, Nostradamus suggested pouring candle tallow into the pot, so as to "degrease" it and make it watertight. These jams, prepared with sugar—a rare commodity in those days—were considered to be remedies and the pots used for their storage were apothecary and ointment jars that supposedly came from the East and Damascus.

Pottery that comes from the earth of Provence, where olive trees with their twisting trunks abound.

These jars were cylindrical, sometimes with a potbelly and a neck onto which a parchment stopper could be attached. They were rare, but a pharmacist in Aix stated that he had "Persian pots containing opium and syrup derivates." These *albarelles* would give rise to a quite varied production, many in faience, as it was more airtight. This was before the Provençal potters decided to adopt what they considered nineteenth-century forms.

Also cylindrical and flat-bottomed like an *albarelle*, they had a broad opening with a rolled edge or a groove in which a lid could be attached. Their sunken walls were decorated in a marbling of red, white, and yellow and the interiors were glazed. They could be sealed with a cork or a tight-fitting lid. These jars were manufactured in Vallauris in six different sizes and several

decorative marbled designs. They were also undoubtedly made all around the Palud-sur-Verdon region.

The preserving jars made by potters from Moustiers were not intended for gourmet use and were "democratized" to the point that they became the receptacle for the renowned and smelly *cacheille* (a goat's-milk cheese). These pots would become ordinary, everyday items that were practical. Farmwomen took to using them because they felt the glazed interiors preserved better than raw clay. For once, porosity was beaten. These pots were airtight—except, that is, for the honey pot, which had a wide belly and two handles through which a string or cord could be laced to tie on a lid. The exterior was raw terra-cotta, while the interior was glazed.

Eastern *albarelles* knew how to preserve the mystery of the jams and jellies they held. Today, unfortunately, we package them in glass jars, shamelessly exposed to the light as if they were in a store window. And now clay pots are only used for dried flowers.

Strawberry Pots

Stored in all these granaries, perhaps the most original piece was the strawberry pot. It was more a container than a nonreturnable packaging. Made in Aubagne on a potter's wheel that was turned using a foot pedal, over the course of the centuries, their production numbered in the millions and then in the 1930s, coupled with a recent interest in our past, they saw a renaissance at the Ravel factories.

This pot, with its broad neck measuring one to one-and-a-half inches (three to four centimeters) in diameter and with a height of about eight inches (twenty centimeters), was made of clay and fired paint. Porous, it functioned like a water jug as the evaporation through its walls kept the contents cool. This pot had a single purpose—to preserve strawberries from Beaudinard and Hyères.

If all that is now cultivated in Hyères is tanned tourists, Beaudinard near Aubagne has not yet aban-

doned its fruit production, a business that dates from the sixteenth century. Concerning the *fraise des bois* or wild strawberry from the Alps that appears in all four seasons, the botanist Duchesne wrote in 1765: "a conical fruit, dark red, exquisite taste." Harvested throughout a good portion of the year, they can treat gastritis, biliary conditions, gravel, gout; remove tartar from teeth; and even erase spots if you should want to rub them over your face. Of course, they must be preserved fresh, at the time of harvesting, and this led to the strawberry pot. Strawberries are slid into the pots and the natural refrigeration process begins. Pots were of different sizes: fourteen ounces (400 grams) for a "Hyères pound"; 13½ ounces (388 grams) for a "Marseilles pound," or about 2½ pounds (a kilo), if one were a glutton or the notary of Marseilles who served Beaudinard strawberries at his Candlemas banquet. In truth, these pots had a good life because, as the saying goes, "eat green peas with the rich and strawberries with the poor"—referring no doubt to Louis XIV's love of green peas. It happens that he also loved strawberries and had great opportunity to eat them, extracting them from these pots during his travels to Marseilles.

The strawberry pot from Beaudinard—where the pottery adapted to local specialties.

Once filled, the pot was placed on top of a gray paper cone, similar to a hennin, and tied with a raffia cord. This created a padding between the pots when they were packed into saddlebags and transported during the night by beasts of burden to Marseilles and Aix. On April 1 along Marseilles's main avenue, La Canebière, a special market would be held for the city's most wealthy residents so they could buy their first pots of strawberries. Then, as production increased, even the poorest people, the porters and the fishermen, could afford to buy them. These facts are known, as there existed a city tax for putting strawberries into the pots, and the quantity never stopped increasing.

Even quarantined ships headed toward the Frioul Islands would receive visits from Marseilles boats provi-

sioned with everything, especially strawberry pots. Once the fruit was eaten, the nonreturnable pots were tossed in the sea. Today, divers retrieve them, often intact and hardened into concrete. At least they don't bring up the pots that, once empty, were used as octopus traps.

The strawberry pot continued to be broadly manufactured until 1930, when it was replaced with baskets that could hold about two pounds (one kilogram), similar to those used today. Lost is the cool freshness of the pots.

The Ravel potters have once again begun producing strawberry pots at the behest of marketers who wanted to offer Beaudinard strawberries in a pot as a luxury item.

Cooking in Clay

To begin . . . with the beginnings: preparation, which is to say chopping, crushing, and straining. The poorer the kitchen, the more work there was. Peace in the household depended on it. Women needed to be highly imaginative with the cooking to get the most from their meager provisions. They also needed tools, and a potter, ever the cook's friend, knew how to make them.

The Clay Mortar

"With the same chisel, he carves funerary crosses and mortars for making aioli . . .," wrote Marcel Pagnol. But this mortar was smooth and heavy and made from marble. Beautiful, yet a little cold, almost medical.

The mortar used in the Provençal kitchen was made of clay, as it had been since ancient times. The potter, who had to consider every detail, as all objects were tools, compensated for the relative lightness of this piece with a clever solution. In order to prevent the pestle

from slipping and the mortar from tipping over as one was grinding, the potter sprinkled some *safre*—the Provençal word for a very fine sand—on the interior walls. It was composed of 90 percent silica and transformed the inside of the mortar into veritable emery paper. Preparation was made easier and certainly no one worried about hygiene. "The mortar always smells of garlic," as one Provençal proverb put it. This was not the case with those made of stone. They were always clean, without any residue. But a clay mortar retained the subtle and stubborn memories of garlic, as well as of oil, the basil used in a *soupe au pistou*, the

The clay mortar— indispensable for the famously creamy anchoïades.

salted codfish that when ground was the primary ingredient of a *brandade*, and the garlicky *rouille* that accompanied every bouillabaisse. In short, the mortar became seasoned like an old pipe, and, above all, it could never be cleaned with modern cleansers. Water is enough. Keep the garlic taste for the next aioli!

Choosing a mortar demands certain absolutes. First, the standing bottom must not be painted, so it does not slide across the table. Second, on all four "corners" of the circle, the points for grasping, each in the shape of half a clove of garlic, must fit the hand. A mortar must be tested to make sure it feels good in the hand. It is said that a stone mortar must weigh about 17½ pounds (8 kilograms) and have an exterior circumference of about 9½ inches (24 centimeters) and an interior circumference of about 8½ inches (22 centimeters). With clay mortars, it is much easier. They merely have to fit the hand. And next, there is the cohort of every anchovy paste: fish *bourride*, garlic purée, and other *rémoulade*, provided you happen to have an olivewood pestle.

Cheese Strainers and *Faisselliers*

"Through the hills of Étoile, he led his herd of goats; evenings, he made cheeses in mats of braided rushes . . ." So wrote Marcel Pagnol to his brother Paul, who made cheese the way prehistoric men did before the advent of the strainer.

In Provence, cheese also had a tradition that was linked to pottery. First, there was the bucket for milking goats and sheep that was manufactured in Cliousclat in the Drôme region during the nineteenth century, as well as in the villages surrounding Nice. A small pot measuring about 7¾ to 9¾ inches tall (20 to 25 centimeters), it had a pouring spout and a handle on one side. These were used for milking small animals that produced only about two quarts (two liters) of milk a day. Sometimes, instead of a handle, a ceramic strip protruded. It had a slit for the fingers to be slipped through so the pot could be felt. No doubt this was to prevent squirting and splashing during milking. Milk was essential to survival.

In olden days, a goat was kept to make sure there was enough milk for the newborn. Herds were so large that they endangered the forests. Around 1730, under Louis XV, the office governing water and forests conducted an inquiry on the state of the woods in Provence, which had deteriorated. It was called the "inquiry on goats" because they were so plentiful and they devoured the saplings.

Once the milking was done, the milk would be poured into a wide-bellied milk pot equipped with handles, a broad pouring spout, and a funnel both for filling

Cheese strainers balanced on the column of a faissellier. Cheese and whey would soon be ready—fresh, sweet, and full of flavor.

other vessels without risking wastage and for letting a child drink directly from the pot as if it were a bottle. Another purpose of these pots was to leave the milk enough time to sit and let the cream rise to the top. It could then be skimmed off and used, for example, in Provence-style scrambled eggs with truffles. These pots were called *biches* (does) and like the milking buckets, were beautifully glazed in yellows, greens, or reds, while the exterior walls were often left raw. This allowed for some breathing and enabled the skimming process to start.

"The costs of packsaddles, for horses and for asses and the other things necessary for a herd: . . . for the

or an extract from artichoke blossoms, and sap from a fig tree, or curds—was added to the milk and then the clay pot was left near the hearth, often nice and hot, in a closet next to an overcoat. Later, the jar would be placed next to the cooker. Curds would form in the belly of the pot, which was protected from the cold, and which kept in its porous walls traces of past fermenting. No doubt today's superhygienic vessels have lost all sense of taste, as aficionados of the past can attest.

Then the mixture was passed through a cheese strainer or cheese mold to let the whey drip out. The strainer was made of red, white, or yellow glazed clay, once again, no doubt, so that the porosity of the vessel would not allow the transfer of any residue of whey to a new batch and so that the taste, if not better, was certainly different. Today, plastic is used.

The cheese strainer was placed on a *faissellier*, a strange earthenware bowl, similar to a *tian*, which had a mushroomlike column in the center. Seven to eight strainers could be balanced between the rim and this "mushroom." The whey would drain down into the *faissellier*, later to be cooked into a kind of ricotta cheese that is still produced in Italy.

These cheese strainers of earlier times were broader and had a larger diameter than the ones used today. The process of separating the whey was much quicker, as the holes were larger. If production was sizeable, the strainers would be stacked in a pyramid, always near a hearth so the heat could accelerate the draining of the liquids.

The cheese would be returned to the strainer five or six times and then set to age, at any rate not eaten immediately with sugar, jam, or salt. Once it had matured for an extended period and had hardened, it would be finely grated and sprinkled on bread and eaten with soup, or on dried vegetables and eaten with eggs. The cheese provided protein at a low cost during periods of penitence. This cheese pottery was important in a religiously observant society—even the poorest people used it for their goat's-milk and sheep's-milk cheeses.

milking pots to milk the aforementioned sheep . . . for the vats in which to put aforementioned milk and to separate the rennet . . . for cheese strainers for making cheeses . . . ," wrote de Barras in his account book in 1480. It was spring, transhumance season for his 34,000 head of livestock—a tide that yielded some hefty, beautiful coins, the color of white silver, by transforming the Provençal highlands into milk, cheese, and ultimately gold.

Freshly drawn milk goes straight into a biche so it can be skimmed.

Aside from the consumption of fresh milk and cream, cheese was most important. Along with liver, goose, and onions, it was one of the few foods that could be preserved in olden times.

To do this was quite simple. Once children, the sickly and the elderly had had their rations of milk, the rest was used to make cheese. A fermenting agent—either rennet

Sometimes the aging went on longer, for example in the preparation of specialties such as the famous *banon*. Here, too, recipes varied. Once the small *tomme* had dried, it was marinated in vinegar and *marc* (a brandy made with grape seeds) and a little pepper, and then was wrapped in chestnut leaves—sometimes thirteen, sometimes six. These packets were then placed in a glazed earthenware jar that was sealed with a damp cloth. The jar would then be placed in a cool room, facing north. After six days, the *banon* was taken out and set on a small mat of woven twigs.

A hanging collection: pitchers, water jugs, consciences, and stew pots.

This process might be repeated up to three times to get the desired quality of a white cheese that could be sliced smoothly and cleanly. A jar well glazed inside and out, and the cheese wrapped in leaves and then sealed, sometimes with a piece of oiled paper, were the only requisites for aging a *banon*. If it is rushed, according to Pierre Magnan, if it crumbles under an Opinel knife, then one has made a *cacheille* (a smelly goat's-milk cheese).

To make this *cacheille*, into a *toupin* (a clay vessel with a glazed interior) were placed "all the remains of cheeses . . . well doused with a brandy . . . mixed until it turned into a cream. . . . It had to be seasoned . . . as one sampled it," recounted Magnan, for whom the *toupin de cacheille* "was a receptacle . . . of great Lower Alpine invention." "There exist some *cacheille* [pots] the bottoms of which have been seasoned for more than ten years," added this gourmand. This is to say that the aforementioned *toupin* must not be used afterward for any other purpose. Author Jean Giono also loved *toupin de cacheille*. "He lunched, as was his habit, on something rather strong, wild onions . . . on the cheese from a pot that it was said he had discovered: Ah! How we've lowered ourselves," he wrote in his novel *Un de Baumugnes*.

The Mystery of the *Tian*

Along with the words *daube* and *aïoli*, *tian is* Provence, its evocation and its great history. But there is no agreement and everyone adds something. For people in Marseilles, Aubagne, Salernes, and Apt, the *tian* was a washbasin. Made of yellow pottery, it was about 12 to 16 inches (30 to 40 centimeters) both in diameter and in height, with walls that flared out. Sometimes it had a spout and two handles. *Tians* could be stacked, which meant they could be placed in a sink and anything could be washed in them, from lettuce, cabbage, vegetables, herbs, to the laundry, some rags, or one's feet. The first known use of the word for this meaning can be found in Achard's venerable dictionary of 1785. "A kind of pottery basin used for washing dishes," he tells us. He added that *rompre le tian* (to break the *tian*) was an ancient Provençal saying that meant to lose one's virginity. The great Mistral (a Provençal writer and the 1904 winner of the Nobel Prize for Literature) confirmed the usage, but with the spelling *tiano*, which referred to *lavo-ped*, a *lave-pieds* in French, or a tub. In short, it was a piece of pottery used for hygienic purposes with a view toward saving water. The *tian* sat in the sink and thus one could easily reuse its contents for watering the plants or as swill for the pigs. In addition, there were

A gatouille *for washing the many dishes used to prepare a meal.*

adise! These pots were also to be found in Aix, where they were used in the preparation of small almond-paste candies called *calissons*, as well as in all the temples of gourmands throughout Carpentras, Salernes, Saint-Rémy, and beyond. For others, the *tian* was a dish for making gratins. Pellas, an abbot of the monastic religious order founded by Saint François de Paule and a gourmet, spoke of the *tian* in the 1723 edition of his dictionary of the liberal arts. In 1839, it was defined as "a meatless stew quite popular [. . .] among the lower classes" made of herbs, dried cod, sardines, or eggs. In the end, the use of the name to mean the container or its contents became muddled as it had with the *patina romaine*. Even dreams of Indo-European origins, or at least Greek ones, have been voiced, as has the name of Virgil.

The pottery would be round, rectangular, or oval, shallow with flared edges, glazed inside and out, but never on the bottom. Sizes varied broadly depending on the number of people in a household. Made in Vallauris, Dieulefit, Cliousclat, and anywhere deposits of resistant clay were found, it was a kitchenware for modest tables. Some producers made a version in the white faience from Moustiers, but the *tian*, with its brown, red, and honey colors, was part of a peasant's kitchen for meatless Fridays and penitence. Theoretically. After all, nothing would keep people from adding to the herbs some spinach, citronella, "Friday foods," an excellent olive oil, cheese, and spices, and then carrying it all in the right *tian* to the bakery. This was the tradition: when all the batches of loaves were finished baking, the women would wrap a *tian* filled with a *tian* in a cloth, which would then be browned in the heat of the oven, with all those flavors and the sweet aromas intermingling. Afterward, one could abstain from meat and do penitence, but not forgetting a glass of wine and some bread.

The potter made a *tian*, and the cook made a *tian* using the not very expensive products, which, starting in the eighteenth century, were to become more and more abundant. Religious precepts were followed while

some that were very large, as well as the *tian-brousson*, which had a hole and a terra-cotta pipe for draining the curds and whey. *Tians* were also sometimes used to measure wine.

The old tian *had a simple, broad shape and innumerable uses in the kitchen and the bath.*

The *tian*—a container, a receptacle, a basin. Today, in Salernes, it is produced using molds or a poured method just as in olden times and is used as a sink for washing one's hands. Humble origins.

Some people used the *tians* for conserving fruits such as plums and apricots, in batches weighing up to some eleven pounds (five kilograms) at a time, before straining. *Tians* would be lined up one next to another and then a plank laid on top of them. Another row would be stacked, as would four or five more—a glutton's par-

enjoying a good meal. There was always something for everyone. But still missing was the fame and glory. Historians would provide it. They report about a pageboy with the formidable name of Zorobabel de Roqueventrouse who was attached to the kitchen service of Louis XIV and was witness to the efforts of the Marquise de Thianges as she prepared, using ordinary ingredients and none of the dignified foodstuff of the royal palace, a dish from her own land of Provence for her king. At this point, historians part ways. There are those who say Louis did not like it, and others who claim that he did. In both cases, they spoke of the *thian* and the *tian*, a usage that dropped the "h." All efforts to find an avowal or any letters of Madame de Sévigné have been in vain. The *tian* remains a mystery.

The vire-omelette, *for flipping an omelet and then for serving it once it has been removed from the frying pan.*

Regardless of whether the origins of this piece of pottery were Greek or not, the recipes made use of herbs and vegetables during spring and summer, when they were most abundant. They also made use of those vegetables that could not be sold. In the baker's oven, or in our modern-day ovens, a *tian* transforms them into delicious *tians*. *Tians* run the gamut from those made of zucchini, to others made of beans, or onions, or bell peppers, or eggplant . . . more than a hundred kinds have been identified. Carpentras or "Tianapolis," the capital of *tians*, even holds a *tian* contest. Best is to buy a range of *tians*. Potters claim that today's *tians*, if made with resistant clay, can be used in a kitchen oven. Furthermore, because they are fired at a constant temperature, there are no longer any misfires. *Tians* can be prepared in all possible sizes and varieties, to say nothing of tastes.

In the past, baker's ovens or ceramic country ovens were used. They were composed of two parts. The first was the base, which held the embers and charcoals, but never live flames. The *tian* would be placed on iron rods that were passed horizontally through holes in the sides of the oven. With several rows of holes on each side, the height could be regulated. The people of Vallauris were specialists in using the oven. The second part was

in the form of a flat half-sphere that capped the underparts. On top was a hole with a cover, similar to that of a *daubière*, through which water would be poured to lower the fire. There was also a *pelle à gratin*, a shovel used to stoke the charcoal. This was placed on top of the *tian* at the opportune moment to make a crisp, flavorful crust. A fire expertise. In those days, people spoke of a "hot, gay, moderate, limp, or lost fire," whereas today we have a graduated thermal scale ranging from one to ten. (Best almost never to use eight, nine, or ten, as they are too hot.) A *tian* should be baked at between three and six (which is roughly equivalent to 226°F and 401°F or 130°C and 205°C), as it takes time for the vegetables to stew. Lower temperatures will also prolong the life of the pot. It must never be forgotten that the cream does not go into the *tian*, but into the oil itself. In the oven, a small bowl of water placed next to the dish will maintain the creaminess of the *tian*, a method practiced with the country ovens and the baker's *buée*. Finally, like the *daubière*, the *tian* must be rubbed with a clove of garlic before each use. After the meal, it must be washed in hot water only. The use of cleansing fluids would cause surface-active biodegradables and nonbiodegradables to penetrate the pot and affect the flavor of the next *tian*.

Vire-Omelettes and *Sartans*

Also called *viro-troucho* and incorrectly referred to as a *friquet* in French, the *vire-omelette* is a star of Provençal pottery and has no true equivalent elsewhere.

As oil goes with eggs, so does the *vire-omelette* accompany the skillet, a venerable piece of pottery in and of itself that dates back to several centuries before Christ when it was used by the Greeks of Massalia (Marseilles). But a clay skillet could not go directly on the flames without the risk of cracking, and thus a person from Provence would make an omelet in a *sartan*, or metal skillet. Oil, also inherited from the Greeks, could easily be heated in it, and to the oil would be added herbs such as purslane, spinach, or Swiss chard, using only the greens. Precious few remains of the Greek clay skillets are in our possession, but was it not Plutarch who said, "Do not spurn at any price cress and oil for an omelet"? This is just about the recipe for the herb omelet, sometimes made with onions, that is beloved in Provence. More recently, Mamé Élise of Aubagne sang a counting rhyme, "The omelet will turn color, when you flip it over." Élise is no longer with us, but her omelet

Stylized curves in yellow glazing, a sign of eternal life.

remains. To prepare one, a *viro-troucho* is the essential partner of the *sartan* if the omelet is to be thick and cooked on both sides, as an herb omelet must be. The *vire-omelette* was the invention of an ingenious potter. There seem to be no remains of any dating from before the eighteenth century when all sorts of things began to appear in Provençal kitchens. The pot was made in different diameters, depending on the intended size of the omelet, and has a short foot attached to the bottom so it

can be grasped with one hand. The top surface is in the form of a flattened cone with a shallow indentation in the center to catch the drops of oil. The cook places the *vire-omelette* on the *sartan* and flips the whole thing over. She then slides the omelet back into the skillet to cook the second side.

In Provence, land of oil, the egg was important. Eating traditions called for eggs to be included with all fish meals, which is to say during Lent and on Fridays when meat was not eaten. This could add up to one hundred and fifty days a year. In addition, cold omelets became part of the diet of the harvester who, because of his long, hard hours of work, would eat five meals a day. Using a *viro-troucho*, one of the crew would prepare an omelet made with onions.

It was a pretty piece of pottery, often with a yellow glaze, the symbol of eternal life, and decorated with a red spiral trompe-l'œil effect, representing love of God and protection. The omelet would be served on the *viro-troucho*—a beautiful presentation even if one does not believe in the symbols. It can do no harm. The *vire-omelette* survives to this day in Aubagne and Cliousclat and can be used for serving a pizza, a tart, or even an omelet (which some people make with artichoke leaves or wild asparagus).

Actors of the Kitchen

Then came the pottery for culinary alchemy. At this point, everything counted: the thickness of the sides, their height, the curves, whether the bottom was flat or rounded, its resistance to heat, the clay, the quick gesture to avoid breakage. These were a far cry from modern pottery where only the firing time varies. In those days, there was the fire and, even more important, the kind of wood. Heat produced from oak is not the same as heat produced from aspen. Also to be considered were the hearth and the cooker with its braziers, which would sometimes be hidden in a closet to protect it from a scavenging cat. Nothing would be wasted, not even the ashes. A long apprenticeship started between

Braziers, sometimes used for slow cooking.

a grandmother and her granddaughter—secrets were passed on, some perhaps dating back to prehistoric times. In a word, knowledge.

Daubières and the Mystery of the String

A pot emblematic of Provence, the daubière is one of the last-born in the family of Provençal pottery. The daube, a method of preparing meat with a marinade and melted lard or fatback, which is then slowly simmered, seems to have preceded its pot. But to tell the truth, no one has ever agreed about either.

It is a fact that the daubière, cited around 1834 in Dieulefit, is the daughter of the round marmite (stew pot), which, in Vallauris, was large, potbellied, and endowed with two beautiful handles and a cylindrical neck. Starting in 1800, it was topped with a lid. But the grandmother of the daubière, or marmite "goutte" with its large round belly and high-placed handles, was a venerable pot from the end of the eighteenth century. And some even speak of a much older ancestor. These "ladies" had the peculiarity of being thrown in reverse, which is to say, the potter began by fashioning the sides, and then redrew the edges toward the center. Once done, he would affix the handles. After some drying time, first in the shade and then in the sun, these "ladies," when still malleable and not fully dried, were struck on the bottom with a wooden bat until the desired shape was obtained! This was called reversing.

In short, around 1850 it seemed that the daubière was about to be born, at least in Vallauris and Aubagne. It was yet to have the stubby handle that would appear after 1850 on stew pots made in Castelnaudary. Furnished with handles attached to her belly, and a neck, Madame Daubière was almost complete with her hollow, stubby handle. All she was missing was her hat. A lid with a reservoir already did exist and was in use particularly on country stoves. It would become the crown of the daubière.

Inasmuch as the *daubière* exists today, one problem remains—the *daube* is more a method of cooking certain meats than a true dish with a fixed recipe. In Provence, everyone claims to have *the* true *daube* recipe—some insist on no vegetables, while others even accept the addition of ginger. And cooking times can range from six hours to seventy-two. Some dictionaries even confuse *daubières* with braziers. The plot thickens. The gourmand Giono made one in a cauldron: "at the Hôtel des Tilleuls in Manosque where Ennemonde went we continued to eat a *bœuf en daube* from the buffet. Three hundred and sixty-five days and nights, he would cook it in a cauldron suspended from the hearth in the room." Was this still a *daube*? Made of metal!

Ultimately, whatever the ingredients, one had to know how to choose a *daubière*. The *daube* must always "breathe" and so it is best for a *daubière* to be only partially glazed, leaving the lower half of the belly and the inside of the lid untreated. A resistant clay has to be used, as a *daubière* must withstand the heat of an oven,

But Madame Daubière is still not ready. Once home, it must be filled with water or milk. Placed upon a diffuser over the gas burner, it is then brought to a boil. This will remove any vestiges of a clay taste that would ruin the *daube*. Then, with each use, it is wise to rub the *daubière* inside and out with a clove of garlic. A magical and tasty hint.

The moment has come to slip in the ingredients. Everything starts with the marinade, which consists of pieces of beef, onions, carrots, a *bouquet garni* (the classic rendition is a bunch of mixed herbs made up of parsley, thyme, and bay leaf), garlic, and red wine. The pot will retain the flavors even after the marinade has been removed and the fatback, fat side down, has been added. There are those who place an upside-down saucer on the bottom as a way to prevent sticking. The advantage of using fatback is that it also gives some flavor and fat to the recipe. The *daube* can then be stirred easily and this precious morsel removed and grilled separately. The meat is then returned to the pot and, depending on the recipe, the marinade as well. In olden

as well as direct flames. When buying one, you should hold it by its two handles or ears to see if it is well balanced. If it tips when empty, could it possibly be carried by its stubby handle when full? The size of the pot naturally depends on the size of the stew. There is no need to buy one that could serve twenty people if you are only two for dinner. One final detail—the lid must be as close-fitting as possible.

days, the cooking was long and slow. The *daubière* would first be placed on the side of the hearth where it was just barely warm, and then slowly the pot would be moved to the center but never placed directly on the blazing fire. The level of the fire would be watched closely, not only to prevent the pot from cracking in the intense heat, but also so that the flavors could gently blend. It was all a matter of simmering and reducing.

Soon enough, the charcoal would need replenishing and the fire tending. An endeavor that would last many hours.

Once the sauce had thickened to golden brown, scoopable with a piece of bread, the moment had come to perfect the daube with a little vinegar and some pepper to aid the digestion. A seal would then be made by placing a slice of bread under the lid. In more recent times, in a mere four hours over a very low flame, this secret chamber would have worked its charms. Some wine would be poured into the indentation of the lid, as well as into the pot, cooling the vapors and filling the kitchen with glorious scents.

Today, when it is prepared on a gas burner rather than in a hearth or an oven, a diffuser or spreader must be placed over the gas jets. Always bear in mind that a *daube* must be cooked very slowly. The vigil begins, which in the past could take up to three days. Once

The emblematic daubière is duly rubbed with garlic before the many hours of simmering.

fully cooked and before completely cooled, the fat must be skimmed off and the stew then reheated. A *daube* can never be simmered enough. Once *daubière* and *daube* reach the height of perfection, they are carried to the table by the handles or ears on either side. This is when the stubby handle comes into use: by grasping it, the pot can be tipped, portions can be chosen, and every last drop of the sauce enjoyed.

Then, a string can be threaded through the small hole at the end of the stubby handle, as long as it is not wrapped around it. Such is the mystery of the string, thick as a sauce.

From *Oules* to *Pignates*, the All-Purpose Stew Pot

Glorious ancestors of the stew pot date as far back as pre-history and continue on through civilized times. First, it was the Greeks, and then the Romans who used them for gruels, vegetables, purees, and soups. There was a point during the time of the barbarians when the *pégau*, a globe-like pot with a handle, replaced almost all other pots. But at the beginning of the sixteenth century, or perhaps a bit earlier, the stew pot began its career. This is not at all surprising, as broths and soups were eaten at every meal. Or almost. They were made from a base of fava beans, chickpeas, lentils, cabbage, and all sorts of vegetables ranging from spinach to onions and squash and leeks. A quite serious inquiry has revealed that this meal had been served at a college founded by the pope in the city of Trets near Aix 354 days out of every 365. Students, masters, and maids all ate this vegetable soup. Everyone had a garden next to the kitchen where *ortolailles* freely sprouted. And then there were all the Fridays when meat was not eaten and vegetables were the main dish. For all these reasons, students of the papal college, as well as peasants and the general population of Provence, used the clay stew pot. This would remain the case through the nineteenth century and even into the twentieth.

As with the Greek pots, these stew pots had a fat, round belly, were globelike in shape, and had at least two handles, more as size necessitated. Some would be so large as to hold about twenty-five quarts or even fifty quarts (25 to 50 liters)—a soup for the hungry masses! The fact is, from the start—meaning at least from the sixteenth century in Vallauris—these pots were made for all sorts of uses and in a variety of sizes. The clay was raw and only the insides were partially glazed; thus the porosity and the "breathing" of the pot remained unaffected. The top of the neck was designed to hold a lid. Its fat belly and rounded base signaled a pot designed for simmering. The heat could be well distributed and the roll of the boil quite even. Thus the cooking was fast, and fuel could certainly be economized. The roundness of the pot also allowed it to be set over the coals on an iron tripod, allowing for an even more precise regulation of temperature. With the simmer under control, the addition of vegetables and dried peas could be timed according to taste—whether one preferred *al dente* or softer.

Starting in the nineteenth century, the bottoms were made progressively more flat as this was what cooks seemed to want. From this point on, the pots could leave the braziers and be placed on the burners of that new-fangled appliance, the stove. Wood was to be replaced by charcoal as a heat source, and thus temperatures could go higher. The cast-iron circular trivets could be shifted and reset, depending on whether boiling, simmering, slowing, or speeding up the cooking was desired.

The marmites *from Vallauris were potbellied and had flat bottoms, to sit better on the cooker.*

The primary concern was the fragility of the clay in relation to the strength of heat. This was so for all pots, regardless of the resistance of the clay. Many modes of approach were conceived.

Before each use, as every grandmother would say over and over again, the pot had to be immersed in water. The air from porous pottery would escape; the rising bubbles were proof positive. Sometimes, several hours of soaking would be necessary if the pot, skillet, *toupin*, or *tian* had not been used for a while or if it was new. Moreover, just before cooking, all pots had to be soaked in very hot water one last time. If the inside of the pot were then wiped down well with oil, all risks would be eliminated. The culprits were thermal shock, splits, and cracking on the flames.

Once these precautions are taken, the *pignate* will adapt to the heat source, whether it is a hearth, a cooker, a gas burner, or, in the case of a *tian*, an oven. A diffuser is essential in a modern kitchen. Pots must be acclimated to changing temperatures. In times past, either the amount of charcoal would be varied, or the position of the pot would be shifted on the cooker. Today, it is the height of the flame or the thermostat that is adjusted. All the same, neither should ever be too high.

Costly in time and patience, cooking in clay was an exercise in imagination. A broth of wild fowl, a *daube* of octopus, grilled meats, and wheat soups were among the savory marvels delicately flavored by the smoke of the hearth—a luxury and a pleasure.

If a cook made a point of using a pot appropriately

sized for the meal, an array of fourteen or fifteen pots, all the same shape but of different sizes, would be in order.

In the absence of a soup tureen, the *marmite* and the *oule* graciously invite you to dinner.

Thousands of Skillets

Writings on cooking, both ancient and modern, have always been very reserved regarding the use of pottery.

Rarely do they specify the kind of pot to be used. There is no word as to which skillet should be used for mackerel drowned in green peas as prepared in Martigues, or for cooking garlicky lamb hearts, or for a fricassee of chicken with croutons in oil and white wine. The fact is, the skillet is wonderful for all recipes that entail browning, charring, sautéing, and the like.

What must always be remembered is to "baptize" the skillet in hot water and "anoint" it with oil before each use, as well as to allow it to gradually grow accustomed to the heat. This is why people preferred "experienced" pots, those that had been used by expert hands and had been seasoned and hardened. People would even repair pots with metal staples so they could be used a little longer. With the prolonged usage, the porosity of the clay would cause minor cracking, covert paths through which the juices and liquids would escape, getting the cook wet. This was the warning sign. The skillet was soon to split. At least the handle would not break off.

Since a skillet is naturally exposed to intense heat, whether it be extremely hot charcoals or direct flames, it must be manufactured perfectly. In Vallauris and other centers of pot making where there was resistant clay to be found, the potter would finish his piece using a metal profile, a tool that compacted the clay so it

With the use of braziers and a more tenable heat, from this point on holding the pot with the hand was possible. The hollow handle remained cool, and thus could be grasped without fear of getting burned. At this time, skillets began to be exported everywhere, not only to the rest of Provence, but to Italy, the Antilles, and Quebec. They would give rise to the Swiss and Parisian casseroles, with handles that were attached very low down. (There are those who say that the *parisienne* came from Sardinia and could not be placed directly on the flames.) Some eleven to fourteen different sizes were manufactured, numbered from thirty to two. Size number two held more than three gallons (twelve liters). Number thirty held a pint (half a liter). There is an explanation for the arithmetic: from a haul of so many kilograms of clay, a precise quantity of pots can be

would have greater cohesion and resistance. If the skillet had been well turned, if it had been properly readied for heat, if the hearth was not too hot, but just right, well handled, the dish would be a true delicacy.

In Vallauris, skillets and *marmites* appeared as early as the seventeenth century. The skillets had a semispherical bottom to help circulate the heat evenly. Starting in the eighteenth century, the bottom would gradually become flatter. It is said that a wooden extension was inserted into the hollow handle for better control.

Skillets, their sides seasoned with aromatic oils, are resistant to even the hottest flames.

made, depending on their classified number, which is to say, size. Thirty indicated that thirty pots could be manufactured, whereas the lower numbers indicated a larger-volume pot, so from a batch of number twos, only two pots could be manufactured.

Once the pots became larger, and thus heavier, they were affixed with an ear opposite the hollow handle. Carrying them was easier, with less spilling. In addition, some skillets had two pouring spouts, particularly those that were used for making jams.

The shape evolved from ancient times, from a frying pan, called a *sartan*, which was used for frying eggs and

fish, to the *châtaignaire* (a chestnut roaster). Because of their fragility and competition from metal utensils, few of these pots have survived.

Cleaning and maintenance remained a fundamental problem for pottery used in the kitchen.

Whether it were a stew pot, an *oule*, a *pignate*, a casserole, or a skillet, the problem was always the same. The material was porous and particles would adhere to it, affecting the next dish. It was at this point that stew pots and skillets came into use for a specific type of cooking. For example, one used for fish would never then be used for meat; there would be one just for game, and so on. On the other hand, a casserole used for rabbit would keep its memories, so to speak, for the next use. Washing it from top to bottom would be a catastrophe. Rinsing it in hot water and scouring a little, but not too much, was enough. This dishwater would then be used for swill for the pigs—nothing was wasted! And only the inside was washed. The smoky residue on the outside would accumulate and seal up the cracks.

There was one risk—the growth of harmful bacteria. True knowledge did not exist, but people had an inkling.

The bottoms of skillets were sometimes perforated for cooking chestnuts gathered in the fall.

Grandmothers' remedies stand as proof. Garlic, for example. The ever-famous garlic. Why rub a clove of garlic on the interior and exterior of a pot? Two preventions are better than one. And this would be done with each use. Garlic came to the fore—it held more suspected antibacterial properties. It was even used against plague. Along with adding flavor to a dish, it served as protection against germs. Sometimes, in the region around the Berre marshlands, people would put cloves of garlic on a burning brick and then place a stew pot, bottom side up, over it for some fifteen minutes for a good fumigation. This was done by those sensitive to the lingering taste of garlic in a dish. Others would douse some absorbent cotton with a white brandy and rub the inside of a pot. Residual odors would be eliminated, cleansing assured, and there would be the added flavor. If a pot, such as a *daubière*, was used only rarely, it would be left to air for two or three days before use. This most definitely was also done with pots that were used for preserving, as the clay would become saturated with the flavors. Could it be for the same reason that today, where people have plenty, sugar is never put into a teapot, a coffeepot, or a dish?

All the same, two or three times a year, earthenware pots and dishes were washed and scoured. Lent was one occasion that was crucial. One must present oneself to God properly cleansed. This period began just before Ash Wednesday and continued for the forty days of penitence in which fats were forbidden and not the least residue was permitted in a pot. The bishops' pastorals repeated the interdiction and were read in church in sermons to the faithful. Using fine ash like a detergent, women would feverishly scour stew pots, casseroles, *toupins*, *terrines*, and plates. Religion and hygiene found communion. The rest of the time, some water, garlic, or brandy would be sufficient.

The lovely terrine. Sometimes rustic, sometimes refined and elegant, but always dignified.

With the cleansers of today, it is much easier. But the "memory" of a pot must always be respected. A platter can be left soaking in water until the oil and particles are gone, and then before rinsing, a few drops of bleach for disinfecting can be sprinkled. Ready once again for more garlic.

The Teapot Turned to Clay

One point that arises in a discussion of pottery is that of lead. It is present in alquifou, a lead sulphide used as sealant to coat pots and the base for decorations. Wood-burning ovens in olden days could not guarantee an even firing and thus some pots would be insufficiently fired, leaving lead residue to mix with the cooking. This also would sometimes occur in pots used for preserving. At the beginning of the nineteenth century, an inquiry called the prefects' report led to reflection on the issue. Potters were asked to use less toxic prod-

ucts and new methods. And this was done, certainly with the more even-heating and efficient ovens. The ill effects of lead were eradicated. In Aubagne, some housewives complained that a certain taste was missing. Could it have been lead?

More likely, with better firing techniques improving the quality of the sides of pots, casseroles, and terrines, different gastronomic results developed, some of which were surprising. It took some getting used to.

In short, an important question regarding terrines was raised beginning in the eighteenth century. Lead was necessary if one wanted to take advantage of the new convenience—the oven. The baker's oven was subjected to tax payable to the lord. The legislation evolved or, rather, became elastic. You had the right to carve an oven into the wall above the hearth of your home measuring "two feet eight inches" in diameter (using old units), which was actually equal to about twenty-eight inches (72 centimeters). Not big enough for baking breads, but fine for *fougasses* (small, flat breads), *tians* and vegetable gratins, pastries, and terrines. At once, the potters of Vallauris developed appropriate pots of many sizes that were round and solid and could withstand the heat. Everything available from the charcuterie and the pastry shop, such as a rabbit and onion paté, a wild boar *caillette*, pork scrapings, and pigeon *provençale*, could also be made at home. Not to mention the *buée* (steam) ovens. At this same time, portable country ovens were becoming more numerous for use in the fields and cottages.

In general, Provençal cooking had its revolution during the eighteenth century. A rise in living standards, new products, vegetables, relaxation of laws, and the arrival of braziers from the cities into the villages all contributed. Responding to the demand, covered terrines grew in number and were reshaped into an oval. The terrine was first found in fine homes and large, wealthy farmhouses before it became popular with the people. Sometimes terrines were made in different shapes, like a rabbit, for example. This was to imitate and then become

"all-purpose helper." The verb *toupiner* means to take care of the pots and do the tidying up. *Toupins* come in all sizes and are for all purposes. They are used for cooking, heating liquids such as milk and herbal teas, as well as to keep a room warm, in which case the *toupin* has its spot at the corner of the cooker. It also had a medical application—it was used against sunstroke. A handkerchief would be placed on the forehead or the head and a *toupin* filled with water would be set upside down on the patient. A grandmother would take care of things and, certainly, it required a special touch. But many people were helped.

The term *toupin* was used for several different pots.

associated with the similarly designed platters found in the country homes of the wealthy. Today, terrines are readily affordable and often more than one is prepared at a time, then stored at cold temperatures. What works well for the heat, does so for the cold. To prolong the life of a terrine, it should be slowly introduced to the cold, never placed directly into the freezer, but first in the refrigerator. Pottery will acclimate.

The family of toupins: for herbal teas, milk, mulled wine, water, coffee, and even, on occasion, magic.

There were round ones with ample bellies that had been made in Vallauris since the sixteenth century and in Aubagne since the eighteenth. Some would hold about six-and-a-half ounces (twenty centiliters), and others a little over five quarts (five liters). Though having their handle and pouring spout on the same axis, they should not be confused with pitchers. These *toupins* were used in the kitchen like a pot, or for heating the milk to make cheese. Moreover, their handle was too small to grasp properly.

Tidying and *Toupins*

Of all the different pieces of pottery, this is the one that is richest in associated vocabulary. The *toupin* is the

The ergonomics of the *toupin* evolved. First, the handle was made larger, so a hand could slip through. Then, in Aubagne at any rate, the pouring spout was moved ninety degrees—pouring no longer required a great effort; slightly tipping the pot would be enough.

The new versions were easier to grasp, with less risk of being burned if you absent-mindedly picked up a pot while preparing herbal teas or heating milk or wine. Some potters replaced the ordinary handle with a stubby one like those on skillets, but in Provence this was rare despite its convenience. Finally, by the end of the eighteenth century, the *toupin* had become straight and cylindrical in Aubagne, and in nineteenth-century Vallauris it was affixed with a pretty handle opposite the spout. The inside was given a coat of colored slip, most often yellow, and the outside, except for the bottom to enhance heat conduction, was glazed.

A broiler pan, to collect the precious juices of meats roasted on a spit.

The many *toupins*—people always had a lot of them—had to be stored, just like the skillets and casseroles. But they were not as solid as our dishes are today. Plates were not stacked. To the contrary, constant care was required to prevent any impact that could cause splintering, cracks, or even splits that would both shorten the life of the pot and lead to unhealthy fermentation. Cupboards specifically made for displaying glassware, pewter ware, and pottery or faience were designed in Provence. Even a poor peasant living in a village farmhouse wanted to display his dishes; colorful dishes, some with decorations, both pleasing to the eye and a source of pride for the owner.

Much could be said about clay colanders, or the fountains constructed in Biot when faience was no longer made there, or the ham-shape casseroles for stews, or the dripping pans lined with a layer of bread to be soused by the juice of the bird on the spit, or the parsley pots, or the baptismal plates, or the bee feeders. So many inventions. The world of pottery is infinite.

The clever parsley pot— how simple to reap the harvest!

The Table at a Peasant Farmhouse

I n the heart of the peasant's kitchen, near the hearth or over the cooker, there would be a set of pottery, along with some metal ware, frying pans, and cauldrons.

Beginning in the eighteenth century, copper pots would be proudly hung and perhaps there would even be a breakfront displaying the pewter. But the essential element remained clay.

The Path of the Plate

The Greeks and Romans were familiar with it, but it was soon forgotten. Well into the Middle Ages, when people were once again becoming civilized, came the invention of *tailloirs*, *tranchoirs*, and the *écuelles à oreilles*, but no plates.

The *tailloir*, as used in the homes of the wealthy, was a rectangular platter with a rim, on which solid foods were served and which might even be made of silver. In peasants' homes, the *tailloir* was made from wood, or even more crudely, from a large, thick piece of bread, in which case it was called a *tranchoir*, that could be eaten. Why bother with dishes? For soups and broths, there was the *écuelle à oreilles*, a sort of bowl with protuberances or

pottery, before local workshops were established, such as those in Huveaune and later in Vallauris.

Soup, which was omnipresent at peasant meals, was eaten as a first course, followed by dishes with sauces. In homes of the less mannered, people used a spoon and ate directly from the stew pot. Perhaps not very appetizing, but how else to mete out the portions? This could become a serious problem, one that could challenge a father's authority and create arguments.

The Provençal bias, which came about during the Middle Ages and would persist until very late, was to separate solids from liquids—thus, the *tranchoir* of bread and the *écuelle* or bowl. Occasionally, the *écuelle* had a small lid that, once removed, could serve as a receptacle for solid foods. The ancestor of our plate, no

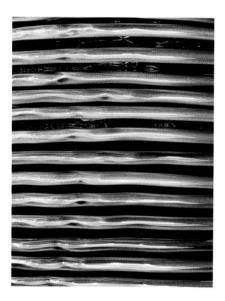

"ears" on each side. The ergonomics are clear: in the winter, when it was cold, the bowl could be taken in the palms of one's hands, the two ears preventing any loss of control when the diner became a little drowsy from the comfort of the table.

And when the *écuelle* was not adorned with ears, it was merely a bowl, albeit one that was often found on tables, as well as in ruins and archeological sites. The bowls remained *écuelles* and were often decorated, as eating was a celebration. This was certainly true of those coming from Italy or Spain, great producers of the

Mountains of plates, flat or deep, yellow, red, white, or even green.

doubt. When the soup was heartier, the meat from it would be served separately—three dishes in one.

Plates made their appearance around the thirteenth century. In fact, the French word *assiette* means a seating or a course at a large dinner. More specifically, the first course, sometimes called in French the *assiette de table* or *première assiette*, became our appetizer. Before indicating the placement of the dishes, the term was used to indicate a guest's seating (or setting). And once again, here was an item that was imported from Italy and Spain. Just as with the bowls and *écuelles*, decorations were either colored geometric, floral, or animal designs, or else religious symbols that were made with the use of a stylet. These items were soon being reproduced throughout Provençal pottery workshops. The progressive refinement of eating habits instigated a rethinking. It would be preferable to serve solids separately, providing there were, in fact, meats and vegetables. In addition, the apportioning of each serving according to the desire of the master of the house could be more easily implemented.

But there was resistance! At the end of the seventeenth century, there were exhortations to be read regarding civility and proper manners. "One must not eat soup from the pot or the platter, but rather, first place it in one's own plate. It is also important to note that one must wipe one's spoon as, after eating from it, one will use it again to serve oneself from another platter." And this was in the homes of the well mannered.

So ultimately, the plate found its place, but it was used primarily for vegetables and meat. The *écuelle* had its heyday in 1653, when it is said that the powerful Cardinal Mazarin introduced the hollowed-out dish for soups and sauces. A rather refined invention, but not too easy to use. If it were used, it was only to be stylish—and then, only in the homes of the noble and bourgeois who had sets of faience for all occasions. Peasants in farmhouses would remain faithful to their *écuelles* for a long time; they knew the pleasure of warming their hands by holding a bowl. All the same, they did not deny the use of the plate—it was well suited for use as a receptacle.

All the same, from the beginning of the seventeenth century, plates started to be manufactured, first in Vallauris and then in Aubagne, Fréjus, and elsewhere. It would not be until the eighteenth century that a distinct improvement in lifestyles would begin. The pleasures of dining would become diversified and people would no longer be satisfied merely to eat and fill themselves. The peasant's table sought to please the eyes, as well as to honor, please, and impress others. Earthenware plates have their place in the setting; next to come would be the white faience plates from England and the factories in Sarreguemines and Lunéville in northeastern France to replace them.

Pottery of Glory

It must be said that such pieces of pottery were not very plentiful. Peasants generally lived economically. Meals would be served in the pots in which they were prepared, and the stew pot, *pignate*, casserole, or *tian* would often be set directly on the table. The advantage was not only that flavors and aromas and heat would be preserved, but also less water would be wasted when washing up. However, even in the most humble farmhouses, as lifestyles progressed, platters would begin to appear.

If a soup had any solids, that is vegetables or meat, it would be spooned into the platter, which served as a

could also be done with faience. These platters were carefully covered with a coat of liquefied clay slip that was colored and would mask the red earth, thus serving as part of the decoration. The platters grew to an almost excessive size—a symbol of the festivities.

Others, called *plats d'équipage*, were enormous, as they were used to serve an entire crew. They were deeper than the others because they would have to hold such large quantities. These were platters of friendship, of men, of equals. No longer an order or preeminence, here was an organized camaraderie where everyone came to eat and served himself, and no one ate directly with his spoon. At huge meals for groups of workers, a community

complement to the plate and facilitated the apportioning of a dish in amounts governed by the status of each individual in the hierarchy. These platters came into the peasant life of Provence in around the seventeenth century. Based on platters bought in Italy, they were made in Vallauris and the pottery workshops of Huveaune. Sometimes they had a simple brown or red glaze; at other times the potter would create a swirling effect. On request, he would create a design, such as a bouquet of carnations, tulips, anemones, and leaves in a vase. Or a marriage scene replete with appropriate symbols.

In this case, the platter became a "marriage platter" used at the festivities and then kept as a memento and a symbol of status. Buying one was proof of social standing, a way to distinguish yourself from the group, which

The luxury of soup tureens with their lids and ever more sophisticated decorations.

bonded, a community of men. There was a community of women that would come together on certain occasions as well. And at these gatherings, people would rid themselves of their jealousies and grudges around a vast, gargantuan meal—an image of a heavenly feast.

"Tant va la cruche à l'eau . . ."

Specialists on questions of water in the eighteenth century thought about the quantities a person should use each day. In an article on the subject in the great *Encyclopedia*, they concluded that every individual should use eight *pintes* (15¾ pints or 7½ liters). This is gallons away from what is needed today. They added, "This is more than sufficient for all of life's uses," which meant cooking and washing the dishes. They were not discussing personal hygiene. For that, there was the river or

the well. People rarely washed themselves during the Ancien Régime or even until the twentieth century.

When one considered that an extended family could

include a grandfather, a married son, and so on, the number of members might reach seven or eight people. This meant that every day between about eighteen and twenty-one gallons (70 to 80 liters) of water had to be carried from the cistern, spring, or well. The water might be near-

by or far off, so vessels had to be easy to handle and not very heavy. It was not as if people were merely getting water for their pastis. Clearly, this need was nothing new, but rather a necessity that dated to ancient times. Such a large amount was, of course, impossible to carry at a single time. In order to fill the storage jar in the house, a pail or pitcher was used and the process would take several trips. From this comes the saying, "*tant va la cruche à l'eau qu'à la fin elle se casse.*" (Literally, "If the pitcher keeps going to the well, it will finally break," but usually rendered in English as "if you play with fire, you get burned.") The same applied to the pitcher that had preceded the

An armful of lilacs in an old pitcher.

jug. The pitcher was wide-bellied, had a tubular neck with a pinched lip in the shape of a spout, and a handle.

Pitchers could always be found in pottery workshops from the Middle Ages up to the seventeenth century. Medium-sized, the pitcher was used for fetching water as well as for serving it at the table. It would be dipped in the storage jar and the water used immediately thereafter, unless it had been filled instead with local rotgut or perhaps even some wine. Beginning in the seventeenth century, the pitcher became more rounded and its belly grew. Its new dimensions generally ranged from six to almost eight inches in height (15 to 20 centimeters), but could be as tall as almost twelve inches (30 centimeters). The circumference of its waist likewise expanded. The pitcher could now hold some ten and a half quarts (10 liters), as opposed to the two or three it handled earlier. Carrying it presented a problem. It was now furnished with a second handle under the spout and a cord would be passed through the two handles. This was then hung onto the saddle of a donkey; or else two pitchers would be hung on a pole that was balanced across a man's shoulders. The wear marks on the bottom of the huge pitchers indicate that they were used at the table. Were people still drinking water?

At almost the same time, the Provençal *cruche* appeared. It had a round belly, one lateral handle, and then a second handle, similar to a basket handle that crossed over the opening. It also had

For pastis or lemonade, sipped under the cool shade of a plane tree.

a tubular spout. This *dourgo* was made everywhere in the workshops of Huveaune, in the region around Salon, and in Fréjus. Its capacity remained relatively small, just about two quarts (two liters), until the nineteenth century when the volume of *dourgo* also tripled. A *cruche* would be filled at any of the fountains that were proliferating. It had a clay lid to protect the contents and could be transported hung by a rope tied to a donkey's saddle or, placed on a cushion, carried on one's head—a pleasant image that would become emblematic of Provence. The *cruche*, like the

the contents could be downed *à la régalade*. This entailed holding the vessel high over one's head and swallowing the fine stream without touching the spout. This venerable method used in the ancient worlds of Egypt, Greece, and Rome, had been preserved by the Catalans and then, at the end of the nineteenth century, was introduced in Provence. Because of its cooling properties and lack of an unpleasant taste, the *kanti* replaced the skin. It was manufactured in Saint-Zacharie and in Aubagne. Original shapes were concocted. In Cotignac, for example, it was

pitcher or *pichet*, was used as part of the table service, as the wearing away on the bottom proves. They were reddish-brown, yellow, or green with unglazed bottoms that functioned like the *gargoulette* of North Africa—in a breeze, the evaporation through the pottery would bring a natural coolness to the water or wine. A certain snobbery pushed some people to have *cruches* that were completely glazed in green to make the owners appear rich. Because it was a rarity, this was a much more expensive glazing, but at the cost of coolness.

Pitchers are placed directly on the clay tiles so they keep their contents chilled.

Among the drinking vessels was one that came directly from Catalonia, the *cantir*, which was rebaptized *kanti* in Provençal. It had a well-rounded belly that could hold some two quarts (two liters), a bridgelike handle that could be grasped from above, a hole for filling on one side, and another very small one on the opposite side, so that

made in a boxlike form, and in Vallauris and Cliousclat, in a return to a symbol of Mesopotamia and Rome, the *kanti* took on the shape of a chicken. Initially a rather utilitarian object, so that everyone in the fields could drink something cool without using a glass or mug, the *kanti* would become a jocular, decorated piece that sometimes even sported a cicada.

Drinking vessels on boats are always risky items, so to diminish breakage, Provençal potters invented the *pichet de barque* (ship's pitcher) which was similar to an ordinary pitcher, but the belly had been replaced by a cylinder that broadened at the base, assuring greater stability even when the boat moved, swayed, or keeled.

All of these objects were highly functional and quite carefully designed. The *cruche* had one handle on top to support the weight when it hung from a saddle, while a second one on the side helped to eliminate any play

during transport; the handle twisted like a basket handle. The spout on the *pichet* was placed rather low

so the pitcher need not be tilted too much to fill a glass, and it was constructed in such a way that it could be easily grasped and the hand would not slip. Also economi-

cal and logical was the *pichet* with a clay tongue in the spout that allowed a stream of water to be poured without inverting the pitcher. It is almost as if it were made to keep ice cubes from tumbling out, but in fact, this *pichet* dates back a hundred years.

A few bits of advice about choosing a newly manufactured pitcher if you want to use it as they did in the past. It should be remembered that the handle of the pitcher was not designed to be grasped, but rather to support the thumb while the palm of the hand is flat against the belly of the pot. The effort expended is minimal, and pouring a pastis becomes a true pleasure.

Cruches with cracked handles that have been repaired with an iron wire or a cord are reminders that to survive, one needed to be frugal. After 1918, these pots would be supplanted by enameled metal ewers and zinc watering cans. *Adieu* to the Provençal belle carrying a clay pitcher on her head. Ewers were now carried from the fountain at arm's length, as people awaited the advent of the tap and the kitchen sink.

Exotic drink services from Dieulefit and Faucon d'Apt.

But the *cruche* would always have its place. First, for keeping liquids cool, provided the pot was only partially varnished. And then for decoration. As for the *pichet*, its purpose remains precisely the same as always—to bring beauty to our tables. Contemporary potters know how to produce magnificent works.

Luxury of Platters

When coffee first arrived through Marseilles in 1644, it was an urban drink that quite quickly became urbane. The countryside was last to succumb to it, waiting until the nineteenth century, and so it is not at all surprising that coffee pots are not to be found of earlier date. And indeed, it appears that Provençal potters did not often make them. Coffee pots found in this region, say in a farmhouse, were most likely made in Lorraine, in northeastern France. All the same, coffee pots were manufactured in Vallauris in nine different sizes ranging from eight and a half ounces to eighty-five ounces (¼ liter to 2½ liters). Each had a lid to retain the heat. Although no

specialty evolved in making these pots, a clear appreciation for coffee in the Provençal farmhouse is evident. Most often, it was prepared *à la chaussette*, literally, "in a sock," the coffee grinds being placed in a cloth sachet and then steeped in boiling water. Drinking coffee quickly became a morning tradition, but an invitation to a cup came to replace a social "drop of red wine" among men and was most definitely a sign of friendship among women. Once filtered, the coffee could be kept hot and always ready to drink. Sugar was generally not used, as much out of preference as politeness: sugar was expensive

and not produced on the farms. It was already enough just to have the coffee. The tradition became so well ingrained that during wartime, people tried to replace coffee with roasted acorns, wheat germ, or other grains, but this was really nothing more than "sock juice." Those moments of meeting and relaxing, the luxury of a short break from the endless hard work of country life, were no longer possible.

The tian *slightly transformed for storing grapes and* panses *de Noël.*

In addition to the coffeemaker or the coffee server, there was a milk pitcher that was similar to a *toupin* and was kept on the edge of the cooker so it would always be warm. It was small, as only a little milk was used to cut the bitterness of the coffee. The two pots would be there, waiting for the guest and the conversation. Initially, these pots were made of tin and later of enameled metal. Although the electric coffeemaker has replaced all this, the tradition of socializing with coffee remains.

Tea and chocolate were left to the wealthy, but a very simple and efficient technique was devised for pre-

serving bunches of grapes to be eaten fresh from Christmastime to springtime.

The pots used for this purpose were made in Biot up until the end of the nineteenth century. They were shaped like cones that had had their tops sliced off; the sides were somewhat thick and six inches (15 centimeters) high, and were glazed on the inside. A vine with a nice bunch of grapes, three "eyes" on each side, and a little resin on the end sticking up was essential. The other end of the vine would be plunged into a pot that had been filled with water and powdered charcoal. Six or seven bunches would be planted like this and then the pot would be suspended from the hooks circling the two clay teats that faced each other on the top of the receptacle. This method was used throughout Provence once the *olivette* grape with its big seeds, or "paunch," had become a part of the Christmas menu, replete with its thirteen desserts. It was crucial to gather vines with hardy seeds so the taste of summer could be relished in the heart of winter, foiling the natural order of things.

The large jar holds in its belly the oil served at the table by its little sister, the burette.

The Burette à Huile

Finally, something must be said about the *bureto* used for serving oil. Stored in a large jar, oil was the foundation of Provençal cooking and eating, and it needed a vessel for serving. This was the *burette*, which was also called a *buire*. The region around Salon and the Alpilles quickly took to olive trees and their oil, and potters conceived of an appropriate pot. The *bureto* was the same shape as a *pichet de barque* (the well-balanced pitcher used on boats) and was made in several heights. The largest, which was used in the kitchen as a reserve, measured some sixteen inches high (40 centimeters), whereas the smallest was about eight inches (20 centimeters) tall and could be used at the table for pouring oil directly onto a slice of bread or into a plate. The spout was narrow, the stream hair-like and, if angled properly, the oil could be poured in individual drops. True, oil had to be consumed frugally, but putting it on the table next to

the salt and wine and bread was confirmation of one's wealth, honesty, and honor.

At the End of the Day

When the day's work was finally done, all that remained for the master of the house was to sit before the hearth, relaxing with his pipe in his mouth. Initially, pipes were imported from Holland, England, and the North. Eventually, potters in Avignon used the Dutch pipes, which were the best, as molds and copied them. Counterfeits. Pipes required extremely pure clay that the women would shape by hand. With an oiled needle, the person shaping the pipe would first pierce it and form the conduit, and then carve out the bowl. It would then be left to dry before being polished with river stones and stamped with decorations. Finally came the firing, which would last seven to eight hours. Once the pipe was removed from the oven, it would be polished with a glaze or some wax to prevent its sticking to the smoker's lips. The success was considerable. All production passed through Marseilles, from where the pipes would be resold near and far. Near the islands in the mouth of the port, in Pomègues, *l'anse aux pipes* (the cove of pipes) was to be found. After 1720, this is where ships would be quarantined. Because of the risk of fire, smoking was prohibited on board, but the sailors did not necessarily obey. When an officer approached, the sailors would throw their pipes overboard—proof that the pipes were not very expensive.

The dream of the poet-potter—a refined, feminine use for clay.

Beginning in the seventeenth century, and certainly during the eighteenth, the pipe and tobacco served as part of a man's panoply on the farm. The pipe would be smoked both at the inn and at home, during the evenings, or when just taking a break and at celebrations. People did not heed doctors' advice: "Bites of smokers have been seen to cause death." This was people's way of confirming the order of things, the hierarchies, the rites that defined everyday life.

Once the pipe had been smoked, it was time to climb up to the bedrooms, each with its chandelier or clay lantern with a candle inside. Beforehand, the embers would be gathered and placed under the *tarasque* (a ceramic damper), shaped like a half-bell with a handle. This was done to prevent a partially burned log from exploding and causing a fire, and also to make it possible to get the fire going the following morning. Woman's work. She, the guardian of the flame and the home. A veritable vestal!

The man would go into his bedroom and the woman into hers, which she shared with the girls and boys, and all the storage jars. A hot brick wrapped in rags was used to warm both one's feet and the bed. At the head of the bed would be placed the *pissadou*, a piece of pottery for nightly hygienic use. Tall and with a broad edge, it had the shape of a sliced-off cone. Some had handles and there was a smaller version for children. Carefully glazed and sometimes decorated with an eye at the bottom, its shape would soon become cylindrical and it would sport two handles. It was also called a *bérenguière* or, more generally, *bourdaloue*, which no doubt was in response to the famous sermons of the Jesuit preacher, Father Louis Bourdalouc (1632–1704).

Women's Work

A perfectly round darning egg. A pure-white egg made of pottery and used as a lure to entice hens in the coop to lay eggs. Symbols of two occupations for women: mending clothes and tending the poultry. For their comfort as they sewed, the women had small, portable braziers into which embers were slid—small heaters for warming the hands.

But their primary work was doing the washing. The white linens included sheets, handkerchiefs, napkins, tablecloths, and blouses. Colored items were few and were cleaned as needed. Doing laundry required a huge terra-cotta basin, which was often fixed in place inside the kitchen of the farmhouse. It would be a good three feet tall (one meter) and had a plughole in the bottom. Sometimes, as with the largest storage jars, the basin would be installed during construction of the house. Two times a year, every spring and every fall, the basin would be covered in a sheet and sprinkled with the fine ashes collected from the brazier under the cooker. Layers of linen and ashes would be alternated until the basin was full. Hot water was then poured over and it would slowly drain through the hole into a pot, to be poured through again. This washing with potash, called *lessif*, would continue for several hours. The laundry was then taken to the washhouse, where it would be rinsed and set out to dry on the grass. To brighten the whites, a pinch of indigo would be added to the water. It is said that this method of washing made the sheets and clothes soft and sweet in a way that our present-day softeners could never equal. And in Biot, they accomplished such wonders.

Taraïettes, Toutouros, and Santons

At Christmastime, in the narrow streets of Meilhan at the top of La Canebière, Marseilles put on its *taraïette* fair with its *santon* figurines. In June, for the Saint-Jean celebration (the summer solstice), there would be another fair where garlic was prominent. *Taraïettes* were replicas of all kinds of pottery in a miniature version, designed to be "used" by the little girl dolls, which were sometimes called *dînettes*. These replicas would be displayed in baskets very low to the ground and within reach of the young clientele. Everything was there, from mortars to *tians* and

daubières, stew pots, casseroles, terrines, jars, pitchers and ewers, chamber pots, dishes, and even moneyboxes.

Sold at Christmas and the beginning of summer, the *taraïette* seems to have appeared around 1872, but some historians try to trace them back to ancient times. *Taraïettes* were toys that served to initiate little girls into their future identity as cooks. It is likely that similar objects had been made earlier, but of perishable materials. Thus these miniatures can be traced back only as far as to the time when people had money to buy them. In other words, potters only began to produce them once there was a market. Their success was so strong, as was their identification with Provence, that there is a tendency to search for more venerable origins.

Today, the *taraïettes* are made in Aubagne and there are two annual fairs held in Vallauris. Some potters turn them on a wheel, but most work with a mold. The success lives on and they are in great demand. Now they are put in showcases, but that is another story.

With the *toutouros* and *trompettes* of the Saint-Jean festival, it's easy to understand the pleasure of returning to the past. It was in the Middle Ages, or perhaps even earlier, that these trumpets were born. Some specimens have been found that date to the tenth century. These were about sixteen to twenty-four inches long (40 to 60 centimeters) and only slightly flared. With time, they became smaller and by the nineteenth century, were no more than eight inches (20 centimeters) long. It was said "the shepherds used these trumpets . . . pieces of pottery like a horn." Although their line of descent is strong, their size did continue to diminish to the point that, today, the trumpets are only a few inches long. Despite having become so small, there was a time when their upturned flare was used to call the girls from the street. Others claim that on June 24th each year, they were used at full blare during the pilgrimage of Saint-Jean-de-Garguier near Aubagne. And they most certainly did make a lot of noise—this is why they were used to ask the gods for wind for threshing the wheat, and also by fishermen at sea, or to attract the girls, or just to be annoying and provocative. These Saint-Jean

trumpets, or *toutouros*, certainly lived up to their reputation. They were accompanied in this mission by the *rossignol*, a sort of water whistle in the shape of a pitcher and named for the nightingale, whose sound it clearly imitated. Properly blown, it could rouse an entire normal-sized neighborhood from its afternoon siesta. Today, replaced by the honking of cars, pottery *rossignols* are no longer sold. Men knew how to entertain themselves, hunting being one of their greatest pastimes, and thrush the preferred game. They would attract the birds during their November migration, from stations built out of fallen branches and set in the ridges along the hillside. The lure would be a "caller," a caged nightingale that had been captured the previous year with birdlime. A sad and debatable practice, as some would say. Or tradition, as others would say. In short, the nightingale would need to drink in his jail. Tiny troughs, identical in shape to the large oil jars, were manufactured and set inside the cage

The art of the santonnier never ceases to develop at Fouque.

for when the bird needed water. These miniature jars measure some two inches (five centimeters) in height, the interiors were glazed just like the large ones, and they served generations of nightingales.

These little jars are no longer in use and no one dares to make them, as hunting has become a reprehensible pastime. But it is still possible to come across one at a shop selling collectibles.

And how can we possibly fail to mention the *santons*, or ornamental figurines? Some small, others large, either molded or sculpted, they could be fancy or from the flea market. They had their own fairs—the most famous were held in Marseilles and Aubagne—but there were others everywhere. Made for Christmas celebrations and the Nativity scenes found throughout Provence, they could be found from the beginning of December through Candlemas (January 6). The home of the *santon* was incontestably Aubagne, where the potter became the *santonnier* or *santon* maker, conjuring up dozens of characters, all drawn from Provençal folklore, in addition to the official figures. Occasionally, literary works would also appear, like those by Pagnol, as well as the *Pastorales*, theatrical presentations performed in the Provençal language that recounted the Nativity as it was interpreted in that part of the world. There was the *ravi*, the *pistachié*, the *boumian* or bohemian (about the shepherd who lost his dog), and many others. Quite a crowd. A lively tradi-

tion that continuously grew richer and was to be found at the ever-proliferating markets of Provence, such as in Aix, Toulon, and Carpentras. But it must be said that although they seem so deeply

A voluptuous round melon dish or mystère *in yellow pottery.*

rooted in the past, the first *santon* fair was held in Marseilles around 1803. There had been some attempts earlier, but the revolution fought against the *santons*. The *santonniers* of Aubagne date from the second half of the nineteenth century. Marius Vassal and François Poulet, known as "Pinto," were among the first. Thérèse Neveu, "creator of the modern-day *santon*," as she was called, created some seventy characters, among them Margarido, the fisherwoman, the lady with the vegetables,

Gustin and his goose, Bartoumieu and the *farandoles*. Thérèse, through her taste, sensitivity, and imagination, would be the kingpin of the Clastres workshop. Other women in the profession were the Gastine sisters and Delepiane, a painter of *santons* who worked for them. And then there were the great number of workshops that emerged and began selling their figurines throughout the world. Even today, Mireille Fouque's inspiration is nourished from the ancestral know-how that reawakens each admirer's buried images, suppressed feelings, and remnants of nostalgia.

Oddities and Curiosities

Beyond the *daubière* and the *vire-omelette*, there were several pieces of Provençal pottery that were odd, like the *pot à escargots*. As in the cuisine of all poor people, nothing could be rejected, not even a snail. The pot was used to "starve" the snails, particularly those gathered in the fall, as they would have had time to feed. The process took some fifteen days. The pot was about fifteen and a half inches (almost forty centimeters) tall, had aeration holes and a lid. Some were glazed and had handles. They were made in Aubagne or around Vallauris.

Portrait of a young cock from Dieulefit

Also to be found in Aubagne was the *fourmeto* or a sugarloaf pan. This was a mold into which melted sugar was poured to satisfy the nineteenth-century sweet tooths of Marseilles. There were also the columbaria or pigeonholes in which nests could be built, the pot for crayfish from Sorgues, the cricket-cage lucky charm, and many other objects. And then the *porte-cuiller* (a highly decorated mug for holding spoons), which was rather rare in Provence.

A full range of pottery existed, answering the needs of peasant life, which was inventive and always in search of beautiful shapes, colors, and decorations. Once it was possible, once essential needs had been addressed, the pottery became decorative and would be displayed or hung up to be appreciated. Proud, dignified, beautiful, this pottery is far from a new discovery.

Roof Tiles and *Malons*

The Provençal house was one made of terra-cotta. For ages, clay had served for everything from the kitchen floor to the tiles used for wine vats and water basins, and the bedrooms that also served as attics. Not to mention roof tiles, *génoises*, and *faîtières*.

Malons and *Tomettes*

In Italy and Spain, which were both influenced by the Islamic world, decorated tiles were the fashion. Obviously, these tiles were not intended for peasant homes, but rather the palatial houses of the wealthy. The pope's residence in Avignon was done in Catalonian tiles. This was a general term and all we know for certain is that these blue, white, and green tiles with interlacing and geometric patterns may just as well have come from Liguria in Italy. Designed like a carpet, they were to become progressively more sought after by the nobility and by rich merchants, as this tile work was yet another way to confirm and display status and wealth.

The vogue took root in Provence, particularly during the seventeenth century. In Arles, as elsewhere, private

lages had their own—to the point where people complained that the forests were being threatened by the consumption of wood. But what to do? The house had to be floored, and properly. Whether it was a farmhouse, a country house, or a house in the village, and no matter how modest, it deserved to be done with dignity. So people cut and carved and worked more than was necessary to furnish ovens with tiles and lime and *malons*. Every twenty years, a green oak tree would be felled and divided into clumps with twigs, which in time would grow into a trunk measuring some four inches (10 centimeters) in diameter. In addition, there were the faience makers and the potters producing other tiles, like the hexagonal *tomettes* of Salernes. And this began in the fifteenth century.

The ordinary paving tiles found everywhere were

mansions would be decorated with ornamental tiling in a variety of motifs such as flowers, birds, different animals, and characters that were presented in a more or less naive style. The colors were very rich and the figures intermingled. This ornamental work can still be seen in churches and châteaux, such as those at Cadenet and La Tour-d'Aigues.

But if these decorative, sometimes story-telling tiles that revealed the vanity of their owner were not yet plentiful, the square, brown terra-cotta *malon* is seen everywhere, and has been since the Middle Ages.

The number of *tuilers* and *malonniers*—makers of the *tuiles* and the *malons*—was impressive. Many, many vil-

Molds and stamps for malons and tomettes. Pottery extends all the way to the floor.

called square *malons* and were between about eight and ten inches (20 to 25 centimeters) square, the tile varying from village to village. Subdivisions were either halves or thirds. Generally, these tiles were manufactured in the same workshops as the *tuiles* (roof tiles). Aside from Salernes, which was the heart of tilemaking, most other centers, such as La Seyne, Bandol, and Marseilles, were coastal. Like *tuiles*, *malons* are heavy but not of great value, so by manufacturing them near the sea, transportation costs were reduced. *Tuiles* and *malons* were exported to the colonies in the Antilles, lands where hurricanes would destroy roofs.

Along with the terra-cotta *malon*, there were others that were covered in red slip, called *bol d'Arménie*. The

slip mixture made the tiles waterproof so they could then be used for wine vats, sinks, and butchers' stalls.

Sometimes certain varieties were polished and made in an octagonal or diamond shape. These *malons* were sometimes used around the border of windows to stave

off an assault of rodents on their way up to the attic or pigeon coop. The spectrum of colors, in particular the green, indicated the social standing of the owner as well as his aesthetic taste.

And then, of course, there was the *tomette*—the tile most emblematic of Provence. It must be said that they are easy to take care of, are cool in the summer and beautiful throughout the year. But they do take a year to manufacture. Following extraction, the clay is diluted with water and then shaped into balls or *pastons*, which are first left out in the sun to dry and then left for months in the cellar to "rot." The consistency of the paste should be similar to that of soft butter. Once this is achieved, the material is stretched out into parallel strips, dried, and then cut into the standard hexagonal shape with a punch. Finally, the *tomettes* are trimmed. Many special-ties were involved: aside from the *pas-tonneur* and the *malonnier*, there was a cutter (often a woman) who was in charge of the sizing and the imprinting of grooves on the underside of the tile, along with the factory's brand. There was also the *rabatteuse* or beater. After examining each *tomette*, she would give it a shine by rub-bing it twice on a plaque coated with a fine powder.

Malonniers at work, always as concerned with the quality of the tiles as with their beauty.

Finally, the dark red slip mixture would be applied either by soaking the tile in the barbotine, or by pour-ing the slip over the tiles. The first method, referred to as *du tian*, would be performed by women, whereas men would perform the second method, *la colote*. After sev-eral days, the *tomettes* would be sent to the kilns.

Loading the kiln would take fifteen days and then the "preheating" process, which used very dry pine, would begin, with the water from the wood passing through the *tomettes*. This would take several days, and when the smoke had turned white the evaporation process was complete. After six days, the *tomettes* would be fired for thirty-six hours while the heat could never be allowed to diminish. It then took two weeks to let the kiln cool down and another ten days or so before removing the *tomettes*. When the process was finished, a mere nine square feet (one square meter) of tile was ready to be shipped.

Many people believe that *tomettes* first appeared around the seventeenth century. Made of the same granular mixture as the roof tiles, they were about a half-inch (one or two centimeters) thick and on their reverse side were imprinted with a cross, circle, letter, square, or star.

By the eighteenth century, the *tomette* would become larger and thinner. The best ones were manufactured in Auriol, but they were also made in Apt. In 1822, Salernes produced only "faience, fine *malons*, jars, water conduits" and bricks and roof tiles. It was not until after 1850 that the *tomette* would become a specialty of Salernes, when during the latter half of that century it would be home to

tiles in all sizes and colors to be used in kitchens, for the cookers, wine vats, and so on. A kind of "democratization" occured in the tile floorings found in the seventeenth-century private mansions, and apartments were furnished with splendid friezes, tiled fireplaces, and decorative panels that were either limited productions or unique pieces. Those produced at the Bocca and Blin factories were especially beautiful and were exported even as far as Buenos Aires. But today, none, or almost none, are made.

Salernes survived thanks to the *tomette*, an exclusive product that developed when Marseilles had truly become a threatening force. After a succession of uses,

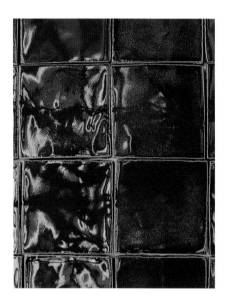  

thirty-seven *tomette* producers. The poor quality of the roads presented an obstacle, but in 1892 the railroad made its appearance and *tomettes* could then be distributed not only throughout Provence, but sent on to Africa, the Mediterranean coast, and Indochina. Wars caused only minor problems, as the *tomette* had become the least expensive of the luxury tiles. Sometime around 1950 was the advent of the awful *granito* (a colored cement with specks of marble that when polished took on the appearance of granite), which only temporarily dethroned the *tomette*.

For years and years, Aubagne had been a center of tile making, much of it enameled. Manufacturers such as Maurel, Barrielle, and Sicard produced excellent-quality

Mosaic floors— vibrantly colorful and refreshing.

the twentieth century saw the modernization and diversification of production—terra-cotta tiles, tiles made by hand, even firing done in a wood-burning stove, an idea of the baker Polidori. One day, instead of filling his ovens with loaves of bread, he put in some tiles to bake. Soon others, like Sismondini and Trichard, using ordinary ovens, followed suit. They made tiles of all sizes and the open fire created a flamed effect. To reduce the risk of cracking, the larger tiles were made thicker. Some of the bakers continued their earlier professions and, after having cleaned their ovens, would make *pains de terre*, or "clay breads." Sismondini continues to produce *pastons*, just as they had in 1900.

Tile making has always existed. Whether using a mold or freehand, the surplus would be removed with a wire, and from a ball of clay, tiles would emerge. Those made by hand would not exceed eight inches (20 centimeters) in length, as anything longer would risk producing irregulars.

All the same, every tile came to know the human hand, as someone would have to do the finishing work, perhaps beveling of edges. Or the decoration, the painting of country scenes, or the "grotesques" that were a specialty of Moustiers in the eighteenth century, the decorative friezes, the flowers, the geometric designs, and so forth—the enamel terra-cotta products of such houses as Basset, Boutal, Vagh, Brest, among others. *Tomettes* are still manufactured today for the restoration of old paving, taking care to match the colors.

The firing done, the kiln must be emptied and the tiles carefully stacked, in preparation for their finishing.

Pierre Boutal, working with Jean Fraux, a ceramist from Vallauris, instituted a modernized and automated enameling process for terra-cotta tiles using continuous-use ovens. The tiles would be fired and enameled without interruption. Some 18,000 *tomettes* could be produced daily, and colors could be changed upon request. Initially, it was Boutal who availed himself of this process, but the Bassets, an old and venerable name in Salernes, also came back to life. Nothing was ignored, and for the most demanding clients, even Roman roof tiles made from a mold were revived and fired to perfection, as they had been in olden days. Pottery in general saw a revival, with everything from bowls to pitchers to *tians* once again being manufactured.

These pieces were made by pressing the clay mixture by hand into the mold. A new method was used that entailed pouring either the barbotine or sufficiently liquid clay in two parts to create the desired shape. After having been very gently removed from the mold, and after days of drying and hours of firing, and then the enameling and decoration and second firing, a *tian* would be turned into a sink. Truly a painstaking task. Whether made in the traditional way by hand or through more modern techniques, even one-of-a-kind requests, terra-cotta pieces for architectural uses, continue to exist in Salernes. There has been a revival of the old ways, and

anything can be had—made to order according to the specifics of a house, or the desires of a personal aesthetic.

Roof Tiles of Marseilles and Aubagne

The number of roof tilers or *tuiliers* throughout Provence was considerable, with the village factories producing small quantities. Everyone looked to save the wood and forests for local usage. The small size of production was directly linked to transportation con-

straints and tiles were manufactured for people living in the immediate area. There was no specialization, a little of everything was produced, as all that was really needed was the terra-cotta.

In short, roof tiling is a very old process that dates from antiquity, when the tiles were used on chateaux and houses. During construction, the master mason would test one after another as each had to "ring the bell," a replication of the clanging of a goat's bell, as well as be able to support the weight of a man without cracking, so once a year a "walkover" would take place. In addition, the tiles could not involve any liming, which would cause splitting during frosts and thus leaks. Tile roofs were ideal for collecting rainwater that would be channeled to a cistern through wooden or terra-cotta gutters. The weight of the tiles was compensated by a strong girding, thick walls, and a generally sturdy construction—the Provençal house was built to last.

It was said that the *tuile* was designed with one wide side and one narrow, like the woman's thigh used for the mold! A silly fantasy. More serious is the 1828 *Statistique des Bouches-du-Rhône* that was requisitioned by the count of Villeneuve, who was later to become the prefect. "The clay having been extracted, it is then piled up and left exposed to the elements for several months. It is then diluted slightly, spread evenly over the floor and little by little, it is pressed into place with the feet. As the clay mixture is soft, it is applied in a thickness that fits in the wooden molds." The text goes on. "One worker removes any overflow, the other spreads the tiles out in the sun, and when they have acquired the proper consistency, they are then piled up in a kind of square chamber and left under the vault which serves as an oven. The fire is maintained for three to four days as desired. The tiles are taken out of the oven and soon presented for sale."

This was a method that lasted for centuries, but starting in 1850, manufacturing and marketing techniques took a turn. In Marseilles, in the span of forty years, the population grew from 150,000 inhabitants to 360,000. From 1853, the port would also increase, dock by dock, and then the railroad served to open up the city even more. From this point on, Marseilles would be both a land-based and maritime center. In addition, two inventions were instituted: first, the Hoffman kiln, which was far larger, produced a much more even quality, and used coal fuel; and second, the *tuile plate*, or interlocking flat tile that appeared in 1840. These new tiles made it possible to cover a roof with tiles weighing one to two times less than the previous rounded "Roman" tiles. Success was quick in coming. The trademark of nineteenth-century Marseilles was not the *Olympic de Marseille* (the city's renowned soccer team), but its Saint-André tiles, the *plates* that filled ships everywhere, along with its ever-famous soap.

The number of companies proliferated and concentrated their efforts. Tiles were no longer counted by the piece, but by the ton, which would climb to several

Fields of roof tiles bathing in the sun of one of those small villages where an undying gentleness of life reigns.

hundred thousand. Workshops and small factories were no longer sufficient; instead, industrial-size factories using mass-production techniques were required. In one fell swoop, all the small manufacturers disappeared—the Marseilles roof tile became cheaper and modern. Tiles would be imprinted with images of bees, lions, stars, or turtles, but sadly, they were flat.

This continued until around 1960, when a taste for the Provençal style was revived, fomented perhaps by a certain interest on the part of tourists and a renewed desire for the tradition of Roman and non-Roman tiles. Roofs would be flat in parts and rounded in others.

Today, in our age of centralization, there remains the *Société Générale des Tuileries de Marseille*, the *Tuileries de Marseille* and the *Société des Tuileries de Marseille et de la Méditerranée*. Other centers of production existed, notably Les Milles and Aubagne, during Marseilles's tenure, but they either disappeared or were reconverted.

It would be impossible to conceive of a Provençal house without terra-cotta. It was integral to a way of life, providing comfort and coolness in the summer. And always, the shelter of a roof with its delicate and changing highlights in the play of shadows and sunlight.

The "Faience Family"

There were silver platters for the nobility, clay for everyone else—people had their place in society, their status, and some degree of refinement of dining. But a rumor was circulating: it seems that, around the Mediterranean, people were beginning to use some odd and prestigious dishes that sang like a church bell. Dishes made of faience.

Antoine Clérissy: An Exemplary Business

It had already been many years since Antoine Clérissy, barefoot and with a skimpy bundle of clothes and a head full of ideas, had arrived in Moustiers. He had heard talk of the clay deposits, the pure water, and the abundance of wood—everything needed for working the clay. In the beginning, the Clérissy establishment was "makers of *marmites* and *holliers*" and in Moustiers there was even an entrance into the city called the *Porte des Marmites.* Clérissy was not alone, as Moustiers was home to some thirty other potters. He was part of a dynasty of humble artisans that had its origins in the sixteenth century.

France Unsilvered

Not to be forgotten, it was in 1672 that Louis XIV promulgated the first of his extravagant edicts. The Sun King embarked upon two adventures that would require silver: the construction of Versailles and the war with Holland. At first, the silver dishes of the noble classes were used to these ends, and then in 1678 the king would use his own collection. In his *Mémoires*, the Duc de Saint-Simon deplored the loss of the "silver furniture . . . sent to the Monnaie" or treasury, and "perfected ornaments whose luxury had comprised the tableware of all the wealthy and fashionable people." More edicts were to come, such as the one of 1699 following the defeat by the League of

These were courageous and ambitious men. In 1651, Pierre was born. In the way that one refers to kings, he was called "the First" and was the founder of a faiencery in Moustiers. His brother, Joseph, left for Marseilles where he was to do likewise in Saint-Jean-du-Désert. A veritable empire! And the sons of the sons would continue on.

In 1679, Pierre Clérissy decided to try a new process that was already being used in Italy and Spain, as well as elsewhere. This was the application of a stannous (tin-based) enamel to create a most beautiful faience, and not just pottery.

Blue faience with "Versailles" decorations that call to mind the illustrious porcelain of China.

Augsburg during the War of the Grand Alliance, and that of 1709 during the War of Spanish Succession.

The days of dining at banquets laden with silver were gone. Certainly, Louis XIV kept some pieces of silver and vermeil because he was, after all, the king. But no one would continue to live in the accustomed manner, not even the princes. From this point on, for them as well as for the nobility and others who still had enough money for luxury items, faience would become the replacement.

People rushed to Lyon, Nevers, and Montpellier looking for faience. Most in vogue were the blue motifs that resembled the fine porcelain of China.

There was, however, a distinct problem. If it were

poorly fired and the enamel not well glazed, contact with a liquid such as vinegar would produce a rather toxic poison. Makers of faience therefore took great efforts in their preparations for firing and decorating. Pierre was steeped in the experience of his ancestors and knew that all his pieces had to be perfect. He dominated the field, even though there were others who dreamed of stealing his enamel formula—a form of industrial espionage. He needed artists who could decorate large quantities in the style of the day and the Viry family, with François Viry at its head, provided just that. François, a true master of painting who was declared such by the city of Riez near Moustiers, first went to work in Toulon where he met great painters and sculptors such as Pierre Puget. There, he created an "antique style" that was filled with allegorical, mythological, and sacred symbolism. Everything was ready, or just about. The partnership of Pierre and François exemplified the dignified perfection of a courtly art, specifically that of Versailles.

All that remained was to become known, to circulate their marvelous creations. Pieces were always being distributed. During this period, work was well distributed through the several local workshops supplying the neighboring markets with pottery. As soon as a potter created a superior work, or if the clay used were better, more resistant to the heat, word would spread. Mule caravans traveled throughout the region, particularly in Beaucaire, site of an old fair where merchants gathered from around the Mediterranean. Pierre, a wise businessman, was well aware of this and he sent his faience—the most beautiful pieces of which were the large platters, trivets, and apothecary jars—to be displayed in Beaucaire. He was always ready to meet with officers of the kitchen staff and the majordomos from the houses of the wealthy.

From the Saddle of a Donkey to Beaucaire

In the heart of the summer, starting on the 21st of July and continuing through the 27th or 28th, Beaucaire would be host to the Sainte-Madeleine Fair. There were exemptions on duties, at least certain duties.

Goods were displayed in stalls along the Rhône and were organized according to categories. There were sellers of perfume, silk, leather, faience, and so on. These elegant dishes did not sell particularly well, but the fair provided a showcase. As people came to Beaucaire from all over, and not merely from France, but from Genoa, Catalonia, Russia, and the Orient as well, seeking beautiful products, as well as rarities from far-off lands, like those arriving from the commercial ports of the Levant, one could make a name for oneself here. Pierre and his descendants knew how to enter this sphere of commerce. In Beaucaire, businesses collaborated: items would be ordered and items were delivered. Nobody failed to appear, whether he were a butler or a lord. And Pierre, with his platters from Moustiers, fulfilled their expectations. Orders would arrive from his sales venues scattered throughout Provence in cities like Aix, Marseilles, Avignon, and Toulon, as well as in other regions of France from Toulouse and Lyons, to Nîmes and even Paris. Once the first pieces were in the king's possession, everyone wanted similar ones, the king being a model for the nobility, the upper classes, and anyone else with the means to imitate them. It was the king's taste that opened the world to the faience of Moustiers.

As for the art of dining, the French "service" that developed in Versailles during the seventeenth century was to become dominant throughout Europe during the eighteenth century. And in this dominance, faience would be "seated at the head of the table."

Eating Like the French

The chief officer of the dining service, his table program in hand, was like a general in battle. It was for him to distribute the olla pots, platters, soup tureens, terrines, and trompe l'œil plates. He also was in control of constructing the balustrades, pavilions, fountains, tracery, and even, on occasion, setting off the small displays of fireworks. The table was an orchestrated spectacle of decorations and splendid foods enhanced, not with silver at this time, but rather with delicate pieces of faience. A setting or service comprised many courses—anywhere from three to

eight. Each was lavished with dishes that would be presented by a multitude of servants and were arranged in advance by the *maître d'hotel*. The faience makers of Moustiers, Saint-Jean-du-Désert in Marseilles, Varages, La Tour-d'Aigues, and Castellet were all kept rather busy. Shallow bowls, mustard jars, sauce dishes, fish platters, vegetable servers, round and oval serving dishes, fruit "baskets," hors d'œuvres dishes and plates all had to be available for every guest so that each could serve himself at his convenience. The serving staff was there only to set down the platters of food, present the dishes and utensils, and serve the beverages.

A five-course meal with five settings for each would

Faience, still bare of any ornamentation, awaits the talents of the painter's brush.

require twenty to twenty-five different pieces of faience. Dining demanded a large appetite: the appetizers alone might include hors-d'œuvres, soups, terrines, perhaps several of each. At large meals, not including serving utensils, it was possible for a person to use ten pieces of faience. The dessert course alone, which would follow the cheese and would include ice cream, sorbet, creams, jams, compotes, and fruit, could use ten to fifteen serving dishes. No one was obliged to fill his dish; a spoonful or two would be enough. But all the same, dishes were a necessity. After each course, save for the oil cruets, salt cellars, and boxes of spice and sugar, the center of the table would be cleared. This habit harkened back to the time when people were afraid of being poisoned at the table.

Without question, extensive preparations and intensive preparatory discussions between the master of the house and the maître d'hôtel were obligatory. Reverberations of the problems can be read in *Le Repas Ridicule* by Nicholas Boileau and in the financial despair of Molière's *L'Avare*. All this is to say nothing of the formidable reserve of faience that was kept on hand. The Fauchiers, the largest faience makers of Moustiers, and the widow Perrin of Marseilles supplied everything from the centerpieces to the pots (used for serving spicy meat stews *à l'espagnole*) and the terrines that flanked the table.

And let's not forget the plates, pitchers, and platters, the shapes of which were recast from the work of silversmiths. Faience even played a supporting role with beverages, since it was used to make the chilling buckets and the servers in which the glasses were placed on ice. A general affluence, particularly in faience, along with the grand lifestyle of the wealthy and the middle class, and then later the desire of even the humble to imitate the ways of the wealthy, guaranteed an insatiable clientele for the numerous faience makers of Provence. This is to say nothing of the exports to the rest of France and to other European countries and beyond. All this occured during a time when the kingdom of France served as a model for everyone.

The Berain Dictatorship

Nothing great would ever have come about with faience had it not been for the talented painters and decorators. The artists were essential, not merely to manufacture the pieces but, even more, to decorate them. Viry would transpose paintings onto his plates, and sometimes the hunting scenes or biblical images were as large as twenty or twenty-four inches (50 or 60 centimeters) in diameter. These huge pieces of faience were desired as much for their beauty as for the pride of displaying them. The *piatti da pompa* (ceremonial platters) made up in their size for the magnificence of the lost silver.

Faience was made everywhere, such as in Marseilles and Nevers, where inspiration was often drawn from the work of Moustiers because, as it was said, "this faience is

the finest in all of the kingdom." Some pieces were hung on the wall so they could be admired and one's social status declared. Clérissy, lending a hand to Viry, acclaimed his production and helped him to go beyond the simple, naive works that were deemed ordinary.

There was no mistaking it. Wealthy people and members of the nobility would order full services to fill

their breakfronts. As the faience was decorated in blue, the heraldic code had to be used with white representing silver, stippling for gold, and so on. Clérissy also worked for weddings. When two families were to unite their children, the two coats-of-arms would be set side by side. He also worked for the ecclesiastics with their many tassels and bishop's hats. Clérissy addressed the needs of the *petite noblesse*, which had no great status but were wealthy enough to decorate their faience with the family monogram in interlaced initials—even topping it with the crown of a marquis.

And if the clientele were only middle-class businessmen, the decorations would be maritime scenes replete with ships and fortifications and merchandise—because anyone who had money could not be ignored.

Then came Berain.

Clérissy and Viry had created a recognized style, a fashion. Accepted, their
will predominated. It needed not bow,
nor be repeated.

In 1675, Louis XIV named Jean Berain decorator of
the king's chambers and cabinet, giving him authority
over royal pleasures that included the art of dining. And
Louis XIV was a gourmand, perhaps even a glutton, who
loved his table. Berain had other titles: decorator of the
royal navy, as well as of the gardens and the academy of
music. He was a true darling of the king, and even
worked with the tapestries.

Then, through mysterious and somewhat unknown
channels, he came to influence Moustiers. It is known

*The period of Berain
and its magnificent
ceremonial platters.*

that the Grand Dauphin, Vendôme himself, along with
the Gobelins, had taken up Berain and thus he was imitated. Flattering the Sun King would certainly assure a
clientele of a supreme order. And it spread like mushrooms. For Berain, it was "the tracery, in the midst of
which the lovers and the satyrs and the nymphs played . . .
the garlands of flowers. . . . The stew pots and the flower
pots, the water spouts shooting into fountains. . . . The
best-known mythological characters in the midst of these
. . . fantasies . . . the center of the scene filled with . . .
many figures . . . Orpheus enchanting the beasts . . . the
dance scenes of Ajax calling to mind . . . ballet suites of
Versailles . . . , Diana in theatrical dress . . . , characters
dressed in the style of the day." So spoke J. C. Davillier in
1863. Berain knew how to integrate classical stricture

with fantastical lightness, Chinese tradition, a variety of foliage, and even a festive Baroque touch, all of which would lead the way to the eighteenth century.

In no time, this new line saw success. Everyone from the Colberts to Madame de Pompadour, to the Count of Maurepas, to the Grimaldis wanted it. And so did Provençal families, the old nobility, great numbers of parliamentarians from Aix, the wealthy Marseilles middle class who had made their fortunes doing business throughout the commercial ports of the Levant, and the Church. Everyone sought the works of Berain—his connection with the king and Versailles being the drawing point. If one were of the nobility, Berain would place the coat-of-arms at the center of the design. The large platters would be displayed on a sideboard and used for ceremonies and serving, while more ordinary pieces, which would include even the faience knife handles, would be used at the table. This went on for some fifty years, from the end of the seventeenth century through 1750. Works in the "Berain style" were made in Marseilles, Varages, and Tavernes in the Var region, as well as in the rest of France. Imitations could be found in Italy, Spain, and even Holland.

Olerys, Clérissy's Spiritual Son

Ferrat, Chaudon, Nivière, Roux, and Olerys all apprenticed with Clérissy, the master in love with blue, monochrome blue, switched to the grandeur and dignified solemnity of the king and of those who chose to adopt such ceremony. Although elsewhere multicolored faience had been produced for quite a while, it was not to be found in Moustiers nor in the rest of Provence, and anyone who sang its praises risked being marginalized. But more variety, more imagination, were needed.

Joseph Olerys was a traveler and he roamed from Marseilles to Moustiers and even through parts of Spain, a country where the faience was multicolored. Upon his return, Olerys made a decision—he would use colored enamels. Like all great artists, Joseph sensed the coming demise of the large platters with hunting

scenes and religious designs. He instigated a taste for frivolity and fantasy, creating motifs with "groteseque-style" figures and introducing flowers. He would also transform the shapes, modulating circles and ovals so that the edges undulated in a "notched" elegance. After some time and several attempts, Joseph Olerys presented new designs that broke with tradition.

"Emptiness all around, he filled it with whimsically painted *grotesques*," wrote Michel de Montaigne. *Grotesques* had existed since the Renaissance, but Olerys was to reconceive them. Along with the image of an ass playing a lyre, which might have represented some

The fineness of the eighteenth century—a beautiful marquise and floral decorations on this refined ewer.

bumpkin who thought himself to be a musician but instead massacred the music, there were monkeylike characters that came from far-off tales and were magnificently plumed. Olerys presented them as caricatures. He was not from Moustiers, and he watched. He did them all—from imaginary animals, plants, and insects to mythical birds of paradise. He even used images of local peasants with features that were exaggerated but not offensive. There was a hint of the *commedia dell'arte*, with its eye for the slightly cruel. Unforgiving, but tender. Not wicked. Like life. And then there were also the potato flowers, a recent appearance. Mysterious, not well known or understood, it was uncertain whether this

Not only did everyone in Moustiers start to copy Olerys, but also in Varages, Tavernes, and the rest of France from Marseilles to Lyons and Montauban to Samadet. With a sense of humor Joseph Olerys would transpose his odd images onto the faience. Along with a thirst for knowledge, his characters exuded a merry spirit, with no care for tomorrow, looking leisurely out upon the world. The designs of the dishes and plates inspired by Olerys had a certain topical resonance for those who used them, but without going so far as to shock the sensibilities of a baron or countess to the point of unnerving them or worse, causing them, to lose their appetites.

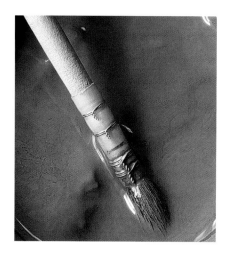

plant—the nightshade—was a food of the gods or of the devil.

There were also the Chinese designs and the monkey caricatures that were derived from objects seen during trips and expeditions to the Far East and the Pacific Rim. Once again, the quality of the work depended on the painter. If a piece of faience were entrusted to a peasant who, just to earn a little money, dabbled in the evening after having worked in the fields, the result was often poor in terms of its artistic quality.

Nevertheless, the monochrome greens, yellows, and ochers called *Beaucaire*, since they were sold at the fair in that town, continued to be produced. Violet monochromes were introduced and their new, festive air was well liked and highly successful.

Beautiful faience demands a talented painter with a fine and precise hand.

But Olerys did not content himself with this vision of things. He was to paint his plates and dishes with mythological scenes replete with flowered garlands. And his references were not only from classical culture. Denis Diderot picks up the story in the *Encyclopedia*. "His Virgins were pretty little trollops, his angels little libertine satyrs or bastards," he said, speaking of François Boucher, the favorite painter of Louis XV and certainly of Madame de Pompadour, who was the favorite of the king. It was a time for having supper in discreet rooms and naughty, bawdy parties for which the meal served as a prelude. The colorful scenes on the dishes were always there as a reminder to the guests of the point of the gathering.

Olerys's creativity and imagination would be a source of inspiration for many workshops that would imitate it with more or less success. Undoubtedly, these copies were intended for a less–well-heeled clientele, which was therefore less demanding but still eager to identify with the noble families, to experience the thrill of debauchery, and to feign the laughter of the *grotesques* in the hope of not going back to that time.

And Olerys did not stop inventing. Aside from his *grotesques* and floral mythological scenes, he also produced monochrome and multicolored flaglike motifs, some of which commemorated the French victory over the English in the 1745 battle of Fontenoy. This was to flatter Louis XV, the king-warrior, who was present on the battlefield observing the fighting that was led by Maurice of Saxony. To eat from these dishes was to imagine the glory and bravery of battle.

Pierrette, the Woman from Lyons

On March 25, 1748, Claude Perrin passed away, leaving behind a faience factory that was in financial trouble, plus debts and three young children. Pierrette, born in Lyons in 1709, who had been his wife and was now his widow, was not one to let herself be ruined and she took inventory of her meager estate.

Flowers bloom everywhere, from serving dishes to vases.

She set off and bought clay, took on some apprentices, and allied herself with Honoré Savy, another maker of faience and a painter. She had no fear of borrowing or of working, and did not stop until her death in 1794. At eighty-five, she was as much a woman of Marseilles as anyone from Lyons could possibly be. A smart woman, with an almost unequaled business sense, she directed her production toward the largest market, without ever forgetting that quality was her trump card—above all, the quality of the painting. Some of the motifs were a little naive, no doubt touching in their clumsiness but likely to put off a wealthier clientele.

Few, if any, pieces of faience emblazoned with heraldic symbols were produced; but rather pieces to be enjoyed for their beauty and to be used in the dining room, as was becoming the vogue in the middle-class country homes, there to be admired. These pieces were

made from the imagination of a woman with a taste for the refined interiors of wealthy businessmen.

There were floral decorations, bouquets with fluttering butterflies and golden insects, or roses, real and imaginary wildflowers, morning glories, daisies, marigolds and foliage, fruits that were painted or molded to form a handle, lids in the sinuous rocaille style, sauce bowls in the shape of ducks, terrines adorned with leopards, dogs, or crayfish on the tops of lids. Sometimes there were vegetables, onions in the bouquets, accompanied by wasps or dragonflies, all in vivid colors, softened by a light, delicate enamel or occasionally a green monochrome with crimson, notched *dents de loup* or "wolf-toothed" edges. Pierrette also heightened her multicolored decorations with threads of gold. Her faiences were illuminations where the light played out scenes with recurring joy. Motifs from Italy and the Far East would be influential, as the business

people of Marseilles wanted to find in their dishes a reminder of the journeys that had made them rich. This was their pride. The beauty of the pagodas, chinoiseries, magots, and curios carried them off on exotic dreams when, on summer afternoons, they stretched out on their *radassier*, a cot kept in an alcove and covered with brightly colored Indian cloth. The precious porcelain that had been named *Compagnie des Indes* had prepared the way,

even if it corresponded more with European tastes than with Chinese tradition. Even if it wore the *chrysanthemum* motif, a beautiful, stylized flower with fringed petals, or the Chinese monkey-figures and drolls sporting conical hats or Manchurian topknots. At a meal, the fun was to let the characters slowly reveal themselves as one emptied one's plate. A refined bonus, a pleasure.

The widow Perrin never ceased being creative. She painted landscapes of ruins, fountains with animals drinking from them, and imaginary scenes inspired by works of embroidery. Sailors also populated Pierrette's faience, always with an air of fantasy, to please the Marseilles merchants whose fortunes came from the sea. Following this line, the widow Perrin adorned her dishes—and she was the only one to do so—with an array of fish, such as scorpion fish, rainbow wrasse, bass, eel, whiting, red mullet, shellfish, shrimp, crabs, and seaweed.

It was the fashion to have a line of faience and this certainly did not escape Pierrette, who remembered the roots of her wealth in Marseilles, the capital of bouillabaisse, which at the time was a poor man's dish.

An ice bowl for chilling glasses; a highly treasured utensil when the sun is intense.

And as the widow Perrin never forgot anything, she also created Masonic decorations, a response to a very prominent convention of the day—the Masonic dinner. There were others who also produced these decorations, but she did so with joy. For the bourgeoisie of the time, who were learned and philosophical and who desired to be such, there was a pride in being one of the "Perfect Harmony" or the "Chevaliers of the Phoenix." Eating from a plate that was covered in mysterious symbols was more than frivolity, it exuded the scent of a plot, almost of conspiracy, between the initiates. The adventure of the fraternity was well afoot.

From Pierrette's factory came the first plates with wavy lobes, some regular and others irregular, ornamental "wings" in an openwork design. She presented an entire set of serving and dining dishes that included round and oval platters with lobed edges in a rocaille style inspired by rocks and shells, which were at once exuberant yet refined. Her services also included soup tureens, terrines

with lids, sauce bowls, bowls, baskets, candy dishes, oil cruets, mustard jars, milk pots and creamers, cups and saucers, sugar bowls, and for the pleasure of it, footed, appliquéd flower vases, potpourris, and pots for cosmetics. There was also a collection of dishes for ice—the bucket for chilling bottles, chillers for individual glasses or for several glasses, and ice buckets, all of which demonstrated one's wealth, taste, and flair for the new. To live the sweet life during the eighteenth century meant new sensations like drinking cold wine from chilled glasses and eating sorbet *à la turque*. Drinking hot chocolate or tea or coffee was de rigueur among the upper classes when visiting or receiving guests. Teapots were displayed and sugar was available for those who wanted it. There was a certain thrill of ownership at the homes of those with exquisite taste, where everything was beautiful.

Marseilles and Moustiers, a Breeding Ground

The widow Perrin had been preceded in Marseilles by the inescapable Clérissy family. Son of Antoine and brother of Pierre, the first master faience maker in Moustiers, Joseph was pressed by the family into the business. Joseph remained in Moustiers and Pierre settled in Marseilles at Saint-Jean-du-Désert, and thus began the Clérissy empire. They would produce vases, apothecary jars, flower boxes, wig stands, pillboxes, and flasks, but few platters and almost nothing for the dining service. Everything was done in blue decoration, as was in the style then. Joseph would be followed by his son Antoine, who was named for his grandfather. Keeping things simple!

Not far from the port of Aix in Marseilles, Joseph's daughter, Anne Clérissy, would found a faience factory with her husband, Étienne Héraud. One thing led to another, and through her daughter Madeleine, Anne Clérissy became allied with the Fauchier factory. Through an administrator that foresaw all, in her will Anne Clérissy "ordered that her heirs . . . get along with Joseph Fauchier . . . desiring that aforementioned Fauchier be preferred over all others." At one factory fountains, candelabras, basins for holy water, and ewers

would be made, while the other would produce washbasins, light fixtures with candles, religious objects, and crucifixes, along with trivets and dining services and even flower vases and olla platters.

The faience maker Gaspard Robert was also related through his mother to the Clérissys, something it seems no one was able to escape. But Gaspard was an artist who was always in search of fluid and strong shapes, like waves rolling on the sea. A very accomplished painter, he loved flowers with bees, carnations, and worked in scrumptious polychromes. His fame was such that it extended as far as Poland, where he sold to "His Serene Highness His Lordship Prince Podoski" thirty-four cases containing five dining services, each composed of eighty-six pieces.

Moustiers, where since the seventeenth century a pleiade of illustrious faience makers have succeeded one another.

Robert had a brilliant and talented apprentice named Antoine Bonnefoy, the only apprentice in Marseilles who was not part of the Clérissy family. That is, aside from the widow Perrin. Sensitive and generous, he would become the representative for compiling the register of grievances for faience makers and then, in 1789, their deputy.

Marseilles would see more than a century of ceramics production having an original form that was to become married to the city's destiny. That destiny entailed an expansion that was linked first to work and intelligence, and then, in 1720, to misfortune due to the plague. More than elsewhere, faience, the art of dining, and the decoration of country homes was understood as an indispensable pleasure of life—the price and fragility of which was known.

A portion of this beautiful faience took to the seas, being sent to the sugar-producing islands in the Antilles, or to the Levant, the East Indies, England, Holland, or even Russia. At this point in history, Marseilles was not merely a gate to the Orient, but to the world at large. And thus it was in competition with Moustiers.

Work went on in Moustiers. After Olerys had died, his assistants opened some workshops in 1750. At first, the Clérissys were present everywhere, their production always being the most important. But the inspiration and

the creative genius were no longer around, although Olerys was imitated. Among the new faces was Joseph Fouque. But escaping the Clérissy influence was not very easy. Just as Olerys had apprenticed with the Clérissys, so had Joseph, and certainly much was passed down to him. Above all, he had learned how to paint. As soon as he could, around 1783, he bought back the Clérissy factory. It was the end of the grandfather. Fouque, this accomplished painter, would only be able to retrieve those pieces that were sold by the Olerys. Finally, Joseph's prin-

cipal innovation was to produce white faience that was just lightly decorated. This would constitute about a quarter of his total production. With the French Revolution having come and gone, and many of his clients having left or been guillotined, he had to offer a product that did not harken back to that past aristocracy. Joseph's descendants tried to institute this reconception. Even his son, Gaspard Fouque, an out-and-out revolutionary, *sans-culotte*, *Bonapartiste*, defender of the Emperor, and royalist, was unable to save his factory until 1852.

There was also Laugier and Chaix who made drinking troughs for canaries, ewers, dishes, baby bottles, bidets, shaving mugs, chamber pots, oil cruets, mustard jars, platters and bowls, pitchers, sugar spoons, fruit bowls, chandeliers, baskets, writing cases, flower vases, creamers, pots for milk and potpourris, and even whistle dolls, salad bowls, shoes, snuff boxes, cups, terrines, and teapots. After the French Revolution, they were two of the sixteen work-

The prestigious reputation of Moustiers faience extends as far as Tunisia.

shops in Moustiers. The revolution had cleaned house.

Before 1789 they were joined by the Férauds and the Berbegiers, who were known for their landscapes, their hot-air balloons, their Masonic platters, and above all, the fineness of their work. Their collection included *plats à illusion*, which were platters painted with trompe-l'œil decorations of fruit, nuts, olives, and more. They looked real and were set on the table during meals to fool any greedy guests who might want to serve themselves. A final warning before the turmoil.

The Ferrats were among the sixteen manufacturers producing in 1784 and were renowned for their delicate, nuanced, charming colors. They would remain active until 1842, but after the French Revolution, they used stencils and stamps.

This host of faience makers had broken away from the Clérissy influence. During the last quarter of the eighteenth century, the clientele had become more diverse and grew to include regular people, travelers, and even seasonal workers on their way to Moustiers. Sales continued to pass through Beaucaire, and the city of Aix, with its nobility and important families, remained a major client. Throughout all of Provence, the reputation of Moustiers remained one of prestige and status. Its producers sold their goods throughout France, but primarily in the south up to Lyons and Toulouse. They also sold them in northern Italy and, on rare occasions, to clients in Barcelona or even Smyrna.

Sweet and naïve designs used by the peasant painters of Varages and the surrounding hills.

The Faience of the Hills

Faience factories became even more numerous in Provence, proof of their success. By the end of the seventeenth century, a certain Gaspard Frazende founded a faience factory in the city of Varages in the Var region between Draguigan and Brignoles, with none other than Honoré Clérissy. A family history that had to be linked with the Armands. With such a kinship, the pieces they produced conformed, or just about, to the line of those from Moustiers. In the eighteenth century, there would be six workshops. Time was the inspiration, represented in images from antiquity, mythology, images of Astraea and Hercules, all in a blue monochrome. Next to come were the *fabriques*, which pictured a character and trees. These simple products came to typify Varages. In addition, there were floral motifs, bouquets, the *grotesques*, carnations, coats-of-arms on platters, plates, bowls, water pitchers, shaving mugs, dining services, and so on.

The Varages workshops also produced *chinois*, but their Chinese-style pieces were more rustic than those made elsewhere. Then, in the nineteenth century, they

confined themselves to the bouquets and to the white pieces, with a few occasional concessions to the politics

of the day. As they were now being manufactured everywhere, faience makers began to mark their white pieces

on the underside to identify the place of origin. The quality of these pieces was never in question. The same clay was used, they had the same brilliance, but producers were no longer, or almost no longer, painting the pieces. They still, however, would chime like a bell when flicked with a finger. These products were less magnificent, less artistic, but on the commercial front, more sensible. New markets began to open up. The clientele, formerly based in the noble and wealthy families, now comprised peasants. Individually, they had less money to spend, but there were more of them.

Piatti da pompa— a melange of love and refinement for pieces used in romantic settings.

Varages was not the only venue in the hills. At the foot of Lubéron was La Tour-d'Aigues and the source of its renown was the Physiocrat J. B. J. Bruny, the son of an eighteenth-century philosopher. The family had become "ennobled" by buying its title. This was common practice during the reign of Louis XIV, who sold the offices. J. B. J., curious about everything, rich and learned, a businessman and esthete, embarked upon an adventure in faience. It was short-termed, lasting only from 1750 to 1785, and with its polychromes and green monochromes was marked by a sense of sobriety. But still, his work did answer the demands of his clientele and included *chinois* motifs, the famous orange monochrome hunting-scene platter, the *grotesques*, and the flowers. But J. B. J. expanded the production of white faience. Following two fires at his château, the first in 1780, the second in 1792 with its ensuing pillaging, everything came to an end.

A marriage box with delicate open-work and colors, at once soft and gay.

Two other villages of importance were Allemagne on the slopes of the Verdon and Brue-Auriac. The latter, not far from Saint-Maximin, was established by a ship owner who had constructed it in one swoop to be a center for the silk, cotton, leather, and faience trades, but this only lasted some ten to fifteen years until, in 1774, it all came to a grinding halt. Other places often mentioned were Tavernes, Avignon, and Goult.

The number of short-lived venues sheds light on what was in vogue, on what was needed, and also on a certain fragility that was at times a consequence of inexperience. Varages, like Apt, would last because of its ardent originality. These were places where, toward the end of the eighteenth century, serious work would begin despite the first kilns having been fired around 1728.

Moreover, Apt had little or no link with either Moustiers or Marseilles, and the effects of the French Revolution seemed not to have been too harsh. The existence of colored clay, of ochers, seems to have inspired the workshops. The signature was the color of

the dishes. This was a more complex, nuanced yellow, with its oranges, browns, reds, and greens that was almost never presented on a white background. There was also the marbled or swirled effect that looked like nougat. While other cities were experiencing a state of collapse, Apt grew after the Directoire (1795–1799) and the Empire (1804–1814) periods because faience was utilitarian, had been designed for daily use, and was being sold at a rather low price. Immediately, there was a broad clientele and the dishes produced were very beautiful. Unlike what had been made in Moustiers and Marseilles, here was a product designed to be used.

White Death

As always in France, as soon as a business takes off, the government imposes taxes. The Royal Treasury started the tradition in 1752, and nothing has changed since then.

As a consequence of development, sometimes the clay deposits ran out and the forests used by everyone from bakers to tile makers, lime producers to sap collectors working for the tanneries, would succumb as well. Even goats could not survive.

The arrival of Dresden porcelain, the "Meissen," which was soon to be manufactured in France, offered dishes that immediately became quite a hit in the finer neighborhoods. Its lightness, transparency, colorings, and fineness explained the elevated prices.

In 1786, as a result of a trade treaty signed with France, the English appeared with a new faience that was cream colored, for everyday use, and was sold for a very reasonable price. Something new and beautiful, this "fine" faience was destined for an average clientele, whereas the porcelain was sought by the wealthy.

And then, in Provence as elsewhere, the French Revolution instigated an emigration on the part of the nobility and a stowing away of money. In place of an aristocracy experienced in good taste and the refined things of life, there appeared the nouveaux riches of the Empire with their uncertain desires. To them, Napoleon offered the production of Sèvres. Moustiers, Marseilles, and Varages had lost their outlets. The factories were closed, the kilns went cold.

All except for the production of white faience. The quality of the production remained, using the same hands, same molds, same clay, and the same methods of firing were employed. But the pieces became simpler. There were neither painters nor decorators, as the first priority was to lower prices to correspond with the "fine" faience. At the same time, this white dishware opened up new markets—specifically, the peasants and

petite bourgeoisie who were suddenly flattered to use services that resembled those that had been used by the nobility. A certain heightening of lifestyle encouraged the production of the white faience.

On June 2, 1839, at an inn in Montée des Accoules near Marseilles, the poet Victor Gelu and his companions challenged the nobles of the Ancien Régime. With forks in hand, a culinary duel was organized to take place in a renovated establishment that would be repainted in white lime and furnished with chairs reupholstered and recaned expressly for the occasion. There were platters for ravioli and others for the piles of tripe and *poutargue*, a specialty of Martigues made from mullet caviar, along with the wine pitchers, olive pots, salad bowls, gratin platters, soup tureens, plates, coffee cups, and so on. And in keeping with the eighteenth-century tradition of colorful meals, the dishes were all in white faience.

This faience was soon to become the only one used. All necessary pieces were made, even cases for sausages, tobacco pots, urinals, statuettes, and vessels for holy water, along with cooking and dining services. The clientele was local and, although not rich, numerous. Following La Tour-d'Aigues, both Martigues and certainly Varages would become distinguished in its production. On the sideboards and display shelves, next to some pieces of copper, these beautiful dishes with their adorned edges and the elaborately curved and multilobed platters would glisten.

Then came the advent of the railroad, which not only brought people to France, but also imported faience from the factories of northern countries. The product was resistant, fine, and decorated. It was the tidal wave of the latter half of the nineteenth century and caused the demise of the few remaining factories. Death, or just a deep sleep?

Yesterday to Today: Moustiers to Aubagne

Faience was late in coming to Apt and Le Castellet, but it would endure throughout the nineteenth century through a series of manufacturers. It was the age of capitalism. Not everyone availed themselves of these

pieces, but the faience makers continued working through the beginning of the twentieth century. Although they had disappeared in Moustiers by 1870, there were almost fifteen in Apt at that time. Their pieces were very colorful, marbled and mottled, used a mixture of clays and nougatine and were enjoyed throughout Provence and exported to North Africa, South America, and the Levant. Good use was made of the railroad in seeking new clientele. Alas, as had happened in Moustiers, the train also brought Limoges porcelain and the industrial faience from Sarreguemines, to say nothing of English products. The business people of Apt did not obey the basic rules of commerce—too much was produced, and the rule was everyone for himself. This all came to an end in 1914.

Fauna and flora inspire the artists.

The unsteadiness of the market continues to affect manufacturers in Varages even today. In Moustiers, there was a certain Marcel Provence, a poet, storyteller, author, president of countless organizations, and founder of the Musée des Tapisseries in Aix. He knew people everywhere. Marcel Provence wanted to refire the kilns in Moustiers, and he succeeded in doing so around 1930 with Simone Garnier who, in turn, had brought in the Gastine sisters of Aubagne and Léon Sagy of Apt and his "earth *flambé*" and in summertime, no less, during a period when the region of Provence was not yet in vogue. The revival was slow to take and did not really emerge until around 1950, and then much more so after 1960 when Provence became a tourist destination.

Following Moustiers, this renaissance came to Marseilles, or, more specifically, Saint-Jean-du-Désert, and was rather extended, lasting from 1921 to 1959. The faience and ceramics that went there to be treated were supposed to be "popular" and used somewhat stereotypical images of detached, brown silhouetted figures upon a sunset-orange background. There were also clusters of pine trees, to say nothing of olives and cicadas, sometimes done in relief and greatly appreciated by all, more than they deserved to be. Decorative objects that were of no daily use, they evoked an idealized image of Provence during the period between the two wars, which was in the

process of disappearing. Nevertheless, in Saint-Jean-du-Désert, they also produced decorative vases in the style of the 1930s with geometric patterns or stylized rose motifs when not returning to the *farandoles* and the *santon* figurines. Above all, in favor of the stronger and brighter colors of Apt and Aubagne, there was a decline in the use of yellows, in particular for the famous bouillabaisse tureen, a 1935-registered design of Saint-Jean. In 1932, there were four pieces of faience: the plate, the lid, the tureen for fish soups, and the plate-sieve for fish. The bouillabaisse, which in earlier days had been prepared in a blackened earthenware

Lavender, with its delicate flowers and shimmering colors also inspires the faience painters.

stew pot for poor fishermen, was now a rare dish, dignifying exalted tables. This because rainbow wrasse, scorpion fish, sea robins, and John Dory were no longer plentiful—overfishing and pollution existed even then. And they were in high demand. Full dining services were needed, as were the plates by Josette Bonneil, an elongated oval platter with a fat fish and some fennel, and certainly the set for an aioli, which had become symbolic of the region.

Aubagne is two steps from Saint-Jean and everything was and continues to be produced there—from pottery to tiles to faience. During the twentieth century, although the art of ceramics never died, the great names did turn their backs on it. Around 1950, the

Isnards, among others, made *fèves* (charms hidden in a Twelfth Night cake), and in 1934, the famous two-sectioned bouillabaisse dish. A short-lived success. They also made the miniatures for dollhouses.

Louis and Théo Sicard were the most famous faience makers of Aubagne. For a start, in 1895 Louis created the cicada design, the insect having been immortalized by the words of the Aubagne poet Louis Neveu, "*lou souléou mi fa canta*" (Provençal for "the sun makes me sing"). He registered the design as an inventor would have and disseminated the image everywhere. The Sicards also thought to produce brilliantly colored, plainly shaped dining services and myriad objects with floral and seedling motifs. They were a part of a Provençal movement that was bent on preserving an image of Provence that never did exist, but all the same.

In the 1930s, the Gastine sisters opened shop and could be seen around Moustiers in the company of Marcel Provence. They produced the *santon* figurines and reproductions of the "Marseilles," services in turquoise blue monochrome, and their sumptuous Art Deco bowls. Not a cicada to be seen, but fantastic images like fish that seemed to be smiling, and also seascapes and landscapes, religious subjects, transfixed cats, and even ashes. This new interest in faience was linked to the explosion of tourism that spread through Provence. The region had its ambassadors, among them Pagnol and Giono. Their Provence was even more idealized than that of Mistral. For the men

When creating a lid, nothing is ignored—delicately worked decorations are added.

who had cloistered themselves in cities but had harkened from this land, Provence remained a necessity.

The end of the war came and now it was Vallauris's turn. The city of pottery. In all truth, faience had been there since the beginning of the1900s, when the barbotine technique was used in making Art Nouveau works with nature motifs. Even then there were tourists. But they were merely seeking some warmth during winter— English people coming to Cannes or Nice. It was the same for the faience makers of Menton and Monaco, who had originated when the producers of Lunéville, Saint-Clémenet, and Sarreguemines had inundated the everyday market. Visitors to these factories only wanted the art of the day, which in the 1900s was termed *art nouille* or "noodle art" by its less informed detractors.

After 1945, it was the sizzling heat of summer that people sought. Vallauris had never abandoned its pottery production. During the 1950s a certain Pablo Picasso settled in the area, and with him came lesser-known artists who would produce faience with influences from everywhere and all sorts of exotic inspirations. People were wild about it. From Massier, in about 1900, to Picasso, and despite some horrible fish motifs and some thankfully anonymous vegetables and provocative pitchers, Vallauris became the center of an artistic faience with its new shapes and colors. There was a proliferation of potters and faience makers who all thought themselves to be artists, even masters, and who were in search of the unique piece that would be more a sculpture than some usable object. This trend not only took root in Vallauris, but in Moustiers, Aix, and beyond.

It must be said that during the 1950s and 1960s, the supermarket culture, with its vast, homogeneous lines and plastic goods and soulless glassware, had taken over. Pottery and faience had little place beyond their past significance. They became the means, in the hands of artists, to bring forth an idea, a dream, the creation of a unique piece. Faience against concrete, fragility against uniformity. And today, Provence remains at the heart of this paradox.

Simplicity and elegance. All the richness of the clay and ocher of Apt are brought into play for this soup tureen.

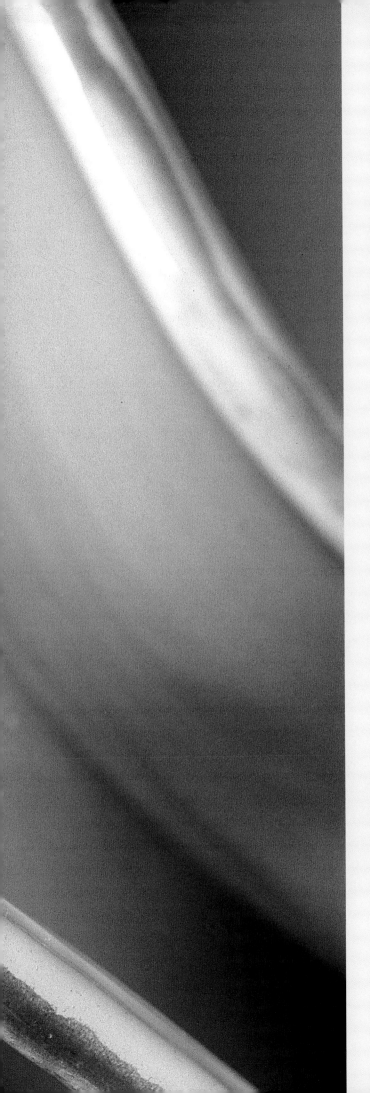

A Bouquet of Potters

It's a kind of magic. With just a clump of damp earth, who knows what can be made? Because clay, this malleable rock, obeys the talented hands of the potter working it. Slowly, the shape evolves, develops, grows between the artist's fingers. All of a sudden, a belly puffs up, or slims down. A phantasmagoria.

Pottery and Faience in the Twenty-First Century

For ages, the potter remained hidden behind his wheel, giving no hints of his existence beyond the smoke from the chimneys and the sheen of his plates. Then, with the twentieth century, fame came to the Richelmes, the Isnards, the Sicards, the Gastines, and the Ravels in

Aubagne. As well as to Jourdan and Foucard in Vallauris. They produced not just pots, but also rounded vases, figurines, and statues. Artistic objects that were both trivial and indispensable, they typified souvenirs created for tourists.

Painting with the "pear." An inventive method that allows for no less than the finest decoration.

And it was the same with the faience. People began once again to turn, mold, and paint perhaps some bird of paradise or a bouquet of buds. A remembrance of the eighteenth century brought back to life by Marcel Provence with the class of Jean des Figues.

Next, it was Picasso and the others who came to Val-

lauris. Today, a throng of potters and faience makers have congregated in Provence. Never have the art of dining and the art of living known such an explosion. Heroes abound—by some accounts, more than two hundred.

The *Cencibelles* of Cliousclat

A June visit to the potters' festival in Cliousclat, there in the midst of the rolling hills, is a must. Situated next to Loriol, this "republic of potters" sprang up, and for centuries people have been working the clay in the many workshops located there. The names of their professions have been just as numerous, with a whole series of terms for "potter," from the modest to the fantastic. In Cliousclat, they were and remain everywhere, in almost every home, as was duly attested to in a 1678 study conducted by the parish priest for the registry office. The clay that comes from there (which can practically be found in the street) has always been known for its quality to preserve flavor, particularly that of milk. Many vessels for both cow's and goat's milk—known as *seilles* and *biches*—were made in Cliousclat.

The Poterie de Cliousclat, a sort of Ali Baba's den for aficionados of Provençal pottery.

One day, just at the edge of the village, a certain Anjaleras came and constructed a huge pottery workshop, as his own had burned down. His vision was big enough to take everyone by surprise. He had his quarry, his kiln, his bowls. Little by little many people came to work at the Anjaleras shop, and like Roman emperors, each had his nickname. They included Grosdolphe, Pelite, Citron, and Arthur (though his name was Pierre). They spoke a language of their own. Their great game was a contest involving hard-boiled eggs on Easter Monday and eating a *salade de Sardes* that consisted of onions, parsley, hard-boiled eggs, and anchovies. All to be washed down with wine because, as they said, "when one is thirsty, the other wants to drink!" Then, with the imposition of tin and plastic, there was a distinct downturn.

Then came the era of Philippe Sourdive. He passed through the odd door, more like a crack, of the

Anjaleras workshop and in 1964, he bought it, along with some other buildings. Philippe was on a quest for a gesture, a trace, and interested in everything—the shapes, the colors. He drew inspiration from potters of other regions, such as from Huveaune and Madame de Fontange. His collections were to become the Musée de la Poterie in Cliousclat. And this is when everything started up again.

Carefully laid out, these pots await firing.

His two sons, Nicolas and Olivier Sourdive, followed him and refired the kilns. There was a renaissance of pottery for the garden, and adornments for the table in red or honey-yellow green. There were platters, vases, dishes, cups and bowls, pots for plowmen, *tians*, spoon holders, and so much else. Locally, the pottery was called *les cencibelles*: there are some three hundred different pieces.

Cathy Sias, Miniaturist

For a long time, pottery was the domain of women. In Africa, where it was born, the wives of blacksmiths held exclusive rights to the practice. Then men took over and chased the women away. In Séguret, with the lace of Montmirail on the horizon and the witches of Tricastin on the wane, Cathy Sias is remembered. Twenty years ago, she traveled to all corners of France before arriving in Provence. She liked everything there and felt it was her land.

Fate left her no choice. She bought a small kiln, had a small studio, a small shop, and made small pieces of pottery. That is to say, extremely small. Even smaller than the *taraïettes*. Pieces that were even too small for some of the larger dolls. She worked her miniatures with a slab on the wheel, as she always turned by hand. Or better said, by fingertips or fingernails, and they had better not be too long! For her artistic decorations, Cathy's paintbrushes had three hairs, and no more than three.

She would work when her soul felt like working, as the pleasure of it all had to be protected. She would do a first firing and then paint her flowers, pansies and

A stunning decoration of braided clay ropes.

dahlias, or arabesques. A gesture or a line would shoot out, and there were curves and interminglings. All personal motifs, sometimes inspired by the widow Perrin, that most beautiful one of the past.

And so came the potpourris, soup tureens, candlesticks, teapots for herbal teas, eared bowls, coffee services, soup bowls, apothecary pots, ordinary teapots, platters, sauce bowls, pitchers, and thousands of other items. All on a scale 1/12th to 1/20th of normal size. Cathy carried her pottery in a sack.

The Man from Tamba

In a hamlet a little below Caromb at the foot of Barroux in view of Crillon-le-Brave on the route to Malaucène,

and not far from Ventoux and the forests, near Carpentras, was to be found a lime kiln. And Tamba, called "the man from Tamba," along with two other potters. Each man worked in his own way. There was also a used-goods dealer and a sundial maker. But, it was Tamba who was like no one else and who is still spoken of with love. His vases, objects, shapes are remembered.

One day, the man from Tamba left everything, abandoning his northern Europe. He decided on a Friday, and was off that Monday. All that remained of his affairs and business was his truck and its meager contents. He took off, not for the west but the south and did not stop until he arrived here. It was April 4 and the cherry trees were in full bloom. Not many people were to be found, and certainly not many clients. But this did not matter, and the man from Tamba built his kiln. He had made a hard-and-fast decision: he would not make things to be sold, but he would sell what he made. The man from Tamba, with visions of Japan and Africa in his head—crazy dreams. He wanted a total commitment. He wanted to knead the emotions in his earth. He wanted all sorts of things.

Extracting the clay from the sandstone, he made stoneware pipes and resistant bricks that he would not fire. He had to grind and knead the clay in order to obtain the rugged, raw material that would be highly resistant, particularly to the potter's hands. A difficult, almost thankless task became a battle as this rebellious clay took shape only after a long struggle. And sometimes, the man from Tamba felt that the clay had eluded him. Using his wheel, he broke with symmetry and created off-center works. There were no second chances—either the pot was born, or it was not. There were few manipulations and the result was always a surprise.

Tamba's rebel pottery—when working the earth feeds the emotions of the artist.

Perhaps a piece would resemble an urn, or a vase might appear to be Neolithic or prehistoric, but it would touch the heart with its naive, yet knowing, effect. But above all, there was its beauty, as soothing as a tale.

Pottery from China

Dominique Reboul put down his suitcase two steps away from Sorgue. In previous times, he had dreamed of Peru, taking photographs and embarking on adventurous trips.

In the end, his flying carpet took him to Hengoat in Brittany where, always an aficionado of things from the past, he became a dealer in antiques and used goods. He then followed the sun to Vauvert and to the courtyard of a large building where, in time, furniture, plows, and all sorts of leftovers piled up under the two split almond trees. Chance presented him with a piece of Quercy pottery that dated back to the seventeenth century. He still has it.

He was then struck by the idea and desire to collect pitchers, *tians*, and all sorts of stew pots from all of France. Varnished and fired clay became his realm of expertise. He moved to L'Isle-sur-la-Sorgue, where antique dealers lived in brotherhood.

This is where he lives today, surrounded, as he has been for more than ten years, by his pottery, originally from Auvergne or Alsace, Allier or southwestern France, and so much coming from Provence, with its vibrant greens and yellows and browns. His shop is filled, he is at home. Dominique has a secret army at his service that brings him his escargot dishes, his *bugadières* from Biot, his fountains, his earthenware andirons, this *vire-omelette*, and that *pot trompeur*.

A fish from the Lomellina—rediscovered and reworked by the impassioned eye of Philippe Beltrando.

Some pieces are rare, some more ordinary, but all of interest to museums, collectors, and the aficionado.

Dominique can set out on a passionate search for some ordinary pitcher or jar, knowing that it is a unique, irreplaceable treasure. Occasionally, in Cliousclat, the "republic of potters," he will come across others like him—there are seven or eight collectors across France who will trace down a figurine, a pot, or an inkpot for someone else in love with pottery. Perhaps one day he will find Aladdin's lamp.

The Massuco *Taraïettes*

The Massuco home is along the roadside, not far from Pagnol country, near *La Reynarde* and the other beautiful homes described in his four-volume *Souvenirs d'Enfance* (Childhood Memories). In the front is a field and through the trees flaunting their autumnal colors can be seen *Le Garlaban*, a jut of a rock. In the courtyard, Tommy, a wall-eyed white dog, frolics, and beyond are the huge brick chimney and the workshops. There is a kiln, a workroom with potter's wheels, and a house. And here are made the *taraïettes*: casseroles, stew pots, mortars, pitchers, and candlesticks, but all in tiny sizes. They are the accoutrements of the *santon* figurines and for little girls to use in their dollhouses. The colors are vibrant greens, golds, and reds. It all started with the grandfather and grandmother. They had come from Italy. He was a mason and she made the *taraïettes*. And so it continues, millions of *taraïettes* identical in all but size to the standard issue. The dining-ware set even includes a pitcher for rosé wine that has a central column for ice cubes. But the Massuco specialty is the *rossignol* whistle, styled after the last ones made in Saint-Jean. The Massuco *taraïettes*, adored from Provence to Japan, are sold worldwide.

The Aubagne Sun

A visitor entering *Chez Barbotine* is first greeted by the cats and then by the smiling Philippe, a man with a passion for gratins, *soupe au pistou*, and Provençal cuisine in general. In fact, he makes pottery just to prepare and present its culinary treasures. He listened closely to his grandmother's explanations of a *vire-omelette*, and he set himself to turning pots and decorating them. Then he began to explore the past. He read about and researched the fish plates from the *Lomellina*, the marriage platters from Huveaune, and the carnation motifs from Sainte-Baume. He took it all in and recaptured it in his vibrant, sumptuous, colorful interpretations. For Philippe, eating is as much a feast for the eyes as for the other senses. Everything starts with beauty.

Chez Ravel

Once upon a time, along the Huveaune River, just steps from Aubagne, there was a factory. It was never huge, but the present-day owners, the Ravels, treat it as if it were. And they have done so since 1837, almost a record. Just like an old country house, the walls are stone and the roof

is red tile. The square brick chimney is enormous. And there, in the corner of the courtyard, is a heap of clay, some twelve thousand years old. Everything is made on site. The clay is either thrown or molded. Some shapes date as far back as 1820. The Ravels even make their own dyes and they do love colors: blues, greens, and honeyed yellows. To obtain the coloring agents, they grind the dyes with sea stones for some twenty-four hours. Then comes the work of the potters, who make everything from dishes for a fine table, to kitchenware, to pots for the garden. Splendid jars, glazed or raw; the prettiest, perhaps, are those with ecru-color sides that catch the sunlight. Pots for geraniums or daisies, or even a lemon or olive tree. Just as long as you do not want some flashy flower like a hibiscus. This is the realm of Guy, Jacques, and Marion, who continue the work of Marius.

The "Stranger" of Mimet

Éric Desplanches was the "stranger" from the North. One day, perhaps it was ten years ago, perhaps a century, he came down from Paris, where he was born, and bought the old presbytery across from the Mimet church. At his

place, life *is* ceramics, and everything from the kiln to the cellar is an indescribable pigsty. The ancient vessels used to collect water from the village square are still there in his residence. Éric works his shop to the hilt, deep into the rocks, far from a sense of futility, close to the subterranean gods that inspired him. Initially, he made columns, basins, lecterns, mirrors, and sometimes even sculptures. Then reconnecting with the needs of people, added to his repertoire cooking utensils, bowls, gratin platters, pitchers with funnel-caps, mysterious objects from upper Puisaye, decanters, tumblers, and dishes. Ultimately, everything required for dining, including soup tureens. He creates his pieces in the color of the night sky, the Milky Way. That deep blue of faraway planets seen through a starlit sky.

In gardens, the famous Ravel jars house orange trees, hibiscus, and other perfumes of the South.

Éric, like his pottery, is a siren. There is no question that he is happy.

Corinne and Philippe, Friends of Montfort

With the double-head of the Bessillons lost in a mistral sky, Corinne and Philippe's oil mill churned away amid the ten houses of Montfort. A forest of oak and pine trees encircled the village. It is a place of scents, with humus and earth wafting through the air. Corinne and Philippe have known each other forever, and have worked together forever. They arrived, as friends, some twenty years ago after a tour through France. Brignoles was a little too big, so they chose Montfort. They knew how to do everything, from stoneware to faience, but Provence remains the land of pottery.

Philippe began to turn his earth red like blood. Coating it with a slip, he only uses colors made from natural oxides, like the ochers used in earlier times, and creates familiar, potbellied, easy, catchy shapes. And Corinne does the decorations. Without preliminary designs, she paints the bellies of the pots with fall-colored leaves and blue grapes. They are as airy and vibrant as watercolors.

Corrine and Philippe do not like to repeat themselves, to make the same pots over and over, so their collections are small. Each comprised only a few copies of any pitcher, platter, ewer, bowl, tumbler, or spoon holder. Their dining and kitchen services are limited. The shapes never cease to evolve, and sometimes, perhaps because the memory of the ancient millers still lives within the walls, they will, almost secretly, make a jar.

Here, there is a dreamlike feeling of calm, of beauty.

The Eleven Skillets of the Saltalamacchia House

It has been almost a century since Placide Saltalamacchia arrived in Vallauris from his native Italy. He was the one who threw the pots, and it was his wife who worked on the slip coverings. They worked hard and from 1920, they had their own workshop. Then, in keeping with the tradition of Italian potters working in Provence that dates back to the Middle Ages, their production continued to grow. The wood-burning kiln was abandoned in 1982, but production went on. After Placide there was first Joseph, and then Gabriel, and today there is Nicole. It is the strength of the family that steers them through the streets of the old village, down rue des Tours and rue du Four, the birthplace of their Parisian casseroles, oval terrines, coffee pots, pitchers, handled stew pots (some with an additional stubby handle, and others that were even round). Today, production consists of *daubières* and casseroles made in a series of graduated sizes and, as in olden days, the skillets number eleven. These are what made the Saltalamacchia name famous. They come in green, honey, and red and can be used as grandmother did for preparing either a nice tomato soup or a *tian*, or a zucchini or Swiss-chard pie. Just as long as it is not something as elegant as veal stew. They also make *barbotines* in the colors of the sun, as well as dining services in Provençal and eighteenth-century styles. They testify to loyalty and the gentleness of life.

The Clay Colossals of Biot

Perched on a hillside, Biot looks at the sea and the jasmines and the lemon trees. Here, much has come from elsewhere: the mimosas are from eighteenth-century

America and the bitter-orange trees are from Italy. These were accompanied by both the potters and their jars. And in 1920 came grandfather René Augé-Laribé. Up until his arrival, the large jars were made from a combination of two clays that were worked on stationary supports. René was the inventor of the cord method of throwing pots.

In Vallauris, the promise of gluttony for a beautiful table.

Very quickly, he felt the powerful appeal inherent there. He sensed that gardens would sprout up everywhere and jars would be needed for all those new potted geraniums and oranges. So with his invention, he set up his home and workshop in the middle of the fields, amid all the future clientele for his jars. He started making them in 1930 and was followed by his sons

and grandsons who were adept at carrying, using the light clay that was a little cream-color and pink, but not too red. This clay does not lend any flavor to what is stored in it, and has brought Biot great renown.

The family came to construct these jars in sizes reaching as tall as six and a half feet (2 meters), clay colossals, all the while maintaining the traditions that been handed down to them. And they resurrected another, embarking on the production of the highly decorated but useful Biot fountains designed for washing hands. These had been made locally from the time of the French Revolution, when Moustiers had stopped producing them. Then there was the ceramic tableware that they made in luminous yellows and greens and white.

Bondil and the Moustiers Tradition

He proceeded with caution in both his words and his deeds. He was the son of a peasant from Moustiers, and it is from there that he drew his sense of reserve and love of the land. He practically lived under the stars of Moustiers. When he needed to provide for his family, Bondil returned to working the clay, the tradition of Moustiers. While Bondil threw the pots, his son and everyone else worked stamping the patterns on the clay. A family business, in the true fashion of Moustiers, where all work was done on the premises. The

At Augé-Laribé in Biot, a rainbow and a work in progress.

mother was responsible for painting the decorations. As was done in earlier times, the Bondils dedicated themselves to faience, but like peasants working in the fields, they also had to deal with the commercial aspect, or management, as it is called today. This was Isabelle's job. The Bondils worked in the same way as the Clérissys, the Olerys, and the Ferrats had in earlier times—as a family. There was a lot of work, but also a lot of passion and pleasure because this is what coursed through the blood of the Bondils.

Their idea was to create a testimonial to all the different periods of Moustiers pottery, starting with Berain's Tempesta decorations and their cobalt blues as beautiful as the Verdon sky. The Bondils then made the mythological polychromes of the Olerys, their landscapes of the ports, their *grotesques*, and their exotic bird symbols of eighteenth-century dreams and chivalry. They also made the *chinois* pieces of the Ferrat days, the balls and Masonic subjects, as well as works from the First Empire (1804–1814) and the time of Charles X. In short, the five great periods of Moustiers pottery history. And we have not mentioned the Bondil flower and butterfly creations. They were very fond of blue monochromes. The Bondils are as much a part of the precious Moustiers tradition as fish are to water. The Bondils *are* Moustiers.

Bondil in Moustiers faithfully continues the Berain and Olerys traditions.

The Blue Monochromes of Varages

For Sylvie and William, craft is a passion. Before faience, it was a haze. Some friends in Biot brought them into the public eye, and once they made their debut, a second thunderbolt took them to Varages. They knew it was all meant to be—fate had guided them.

They remained there, but needed a livelihood. A house was for sale, and it happened to have been owned by a potter who had worked between 1900 and 1908. The potter and his family, the Offners from Franche-

Comté, had inherited the house, which had already been in the hands of faience makers. They were very attached to the heritage, and rummaged around, finding molds for platters in the shape of fish, cocks, and hens that had been made in the Varages tradition of the period between the end of the seventeenth century and the beginning of the nineteenth, the Belle Époque. They were signed by Michel Battaglia, a faience maker who worked at the end of the nineteenth century and the beginning of the twentieth. Battaglia also worked with molds and was himself the heir of Tholosan, a nineteenth-century faience painter. It was all meant to be. William and Sylvie, faience makers of Varages since 1997, would go into the village museum with the idea of enriching their collection, protecting the memory— the heritage.

Faience is their life. When they are not producing, they are studying. When they are not studying, they are decorating. They use old motifs, vibrant colors, flowers, fish, both contemporary shapes and many from the past, and the white style with a transparent tin enamel on the rims. Or else they are restoring molds or scouting about, looking for some more. William prefers the airy blue translucent monochromes that are like a dream, like the dream of his life.

Jean d'Apt

At the Jean d'Apt establishment, faience was a family affair. There have been more than six generations who had "rotted" the earth, made molds, and worked mixtures of the earth: the yellow, green, brown, and red of this strange land where the clay takes on the colors of the rainbow. Jean had inherited his grandfather Joseph's secrets. And along with those, he learned from others in this "Morocco of pottery and faience" of his childhood. When he returned to his country house with its green shutters in the midst of the pines and the plane trees and orange trees, he remembered that everything was within sight and the depths of time. The forebears showed him the way. He then set himself

to making fruit bowls, chocolate dishes, large fish platters, hors d'œuvres dishes, salad bowls, dessert dishes, bowls, soup tureens and candlesticks, vases and teacups, and even ashtrays, plates with daisies and vine leaves all in marbled Naples yellow, so beautiful that

they could be mistaken for nougat. Even blue nougat. Today, residing in the heaven of potters, Jean has left us his dreamlike faience and his dear friendship.

The finess and perfection of a great master, the valiant heir of family know-how.

The Chevalier with the Pipe

Jean-Michel Coquet is a cabinetmaker and painter. And here is how it happened that, one day, stopping in Moustiers, he became a faience maker. His car had broken down, the mechanic was in no special rush, the air was good and so was the light, and Jean-Michel walked around. His friends suggested he make the most of it and relax under the plane trees.

He was drawn to a building, an old electric factory. Not really knowing what had happened to him, he moved in and started making clay pipes. It was an old idea; he found them very elegant, and nobody was making them anymore. His car had been repaired for quite a while by the time he got to firing his first batch. It was Simone Garnier of Moustiers who took in this poor potter without a kiln. In his abandoned factory that had become a pipe workshop, Coquet recognized the numerous inscriptions on the walls and was later to learn that they had been left there by the Gastine sisters of Aubagne, who had come in 1920, at the invitation of Marcel Provence, to revive Moustiers. And Coquet saw that he was on the right path, following in the tracks of the divine Marcel.

But Jean-Michel enjoyed his solitude and he would move to Puimoisson. At that time, in the 1970s, he was the only clay-pipe maker in Provence. Jean-Michel moved once again to Vernègues, where he remains today. At the end of his journey, he is making cutlery, magnificent handles on blades seven times polished, glistening like silver, as well as travel clocks replete with a handle, like those used by eighteenth-century travelers in stagecoaches, and of course the pipes and tobacco pots. He also makes everything that comprises the *art de table*, as well as decorations, pottery for the garden, and even enameled lava, as well as faience eggcups and violins.

Fruit more real than the real, at Figuères. Quite a surprise for the distracted gourmand.

Jean-Michel knows how to do everything because he works with respect. Little by little he has come to resemble the chevalier with the pipe—his insignia.

Platters *à Illusion* from the Figuères Faïencerie

There is an avenue that stretches for some 410 feet (125 meters) and opens onto the sea, the hills of the Estaque dominating beyond in the foreground, pink in the sun. At the end, with its ocher-color walls, is the Figuères Faïencerie, the establishment of Gilberte and Marcel, two rather passionate people. They have been here for forty years. In the beginning, they made dishes and ceramic jewelry. Their passion pushed them on, and in their quest, they came upon *trompe-l'œil* and *plats à illusion*, those platters with optical-illusion motifs. They followed the trail that led from the bizarre sixteenth-century painter Arcimboldo to Bernard Palissy to the eighteenth-century Charles Hannong from Strasbourg to the Clérissys, and finally to the Ferrats. They have created a collection of some eighty replicas of fruits, vegetables, and mushrooms that they combine with plates, cups, fruit baskets, fruit bowls, and platters—thousands of possible marriages, both in colors and in white. Today, like Maître Panisse, the veil merchant, Marcel and Gilberte could rename their business Figuères et Fils, as their two sons, Robert and Éric, now work there.

There is a corner where the molds are made. The molds are used only a few dozen times each, so as to preserve freshness. There is the room with the kiln, and then also the laboratory with its notebooks filled with formulas and recipes, as Marcel is always researching something new. Finally, there is the area for painting, where they strive to achieve a transparency and warmth of color, as if the light were radiating from within the fruit. Along with the platters and dishes of the widow Perrin, marvels of refinement. Entering their shop is magical—it's as beautiful as a Cézanne painting.

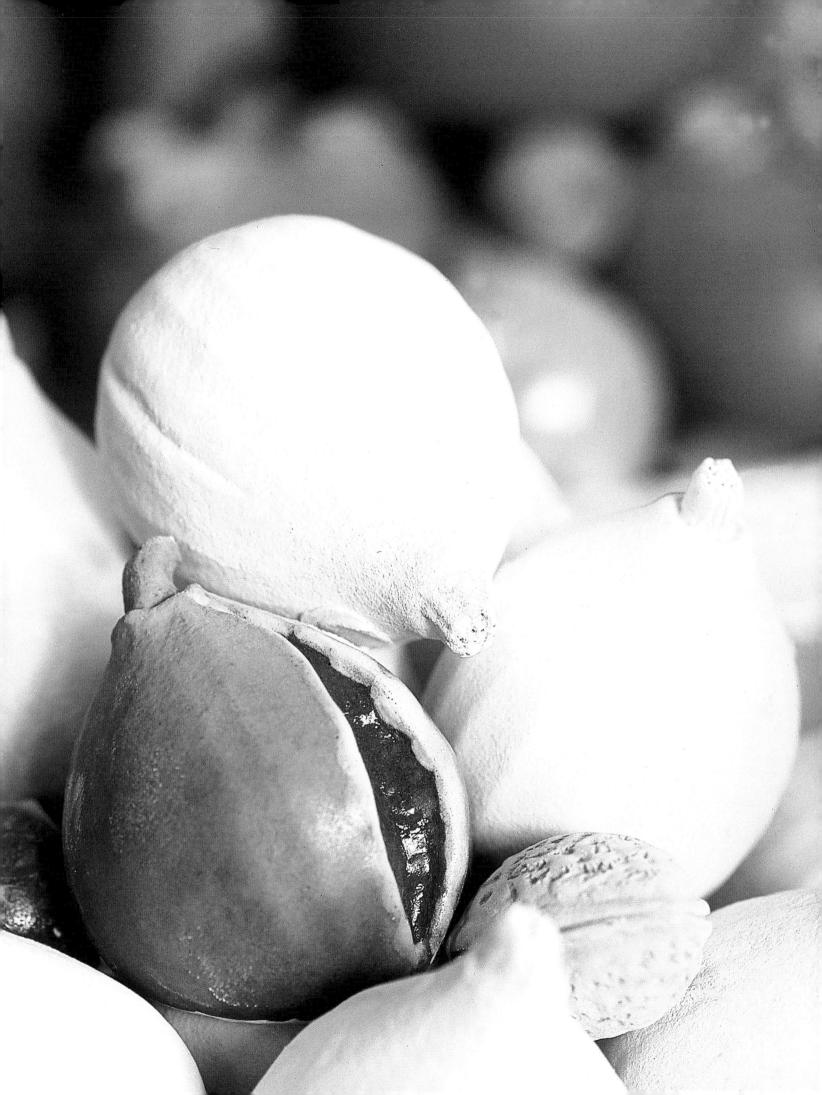

Profession: Ceramics Repairer

Perrine Thoumyre lived in the flat land around Arles. All her life, she had watched her parents work on faience, making repairs using a glue made from rabbit skin and staples from the strong ribs of umbrellas, just as they had done in the old days. Perrine sought tranquillity and beauty and she went to Oppède in that mysterious region of Lubéron, full of secrets. She settled there, rebuilt her house, and decided to continue the work of her parents—repairers of faience and porcelain. She knew how to paint and draw and, of course, had the treasure of her father's experience. She observed, looking to rediscover the hand of the faience maker, the gesture, the stroke of the Ferrats, the Olerys, the

widow Perrin, and the Clérissys. Perrine would discover very quickly that each piece, with all its cracks, had to be *Every piece is a wellspring.* respected. She had to be everything from a chemist to a surgeon and a painter, but more, she had to be inside the mind of the gesture at the moment an object was born. Above all, she needed humility. And this is how she learned to restore plates, soup tureens, and those most delicate dishes used for chilling. There was also the restoration of the *illusion* pieces, something no longer to be seen, which entailed keeping within an object, always on its own terms. Perrine worked with antique dealers from Nice to Brittany and from Spain to New York, as well as with museums and for all those aficionados mad about faience.

Sometimes a funeral urn broken in two would arrive at her shop, complete with ashes. Or a Mayan platter on which the hearts of young girls were offered in sacrifice to the gods. Every dish has its history.

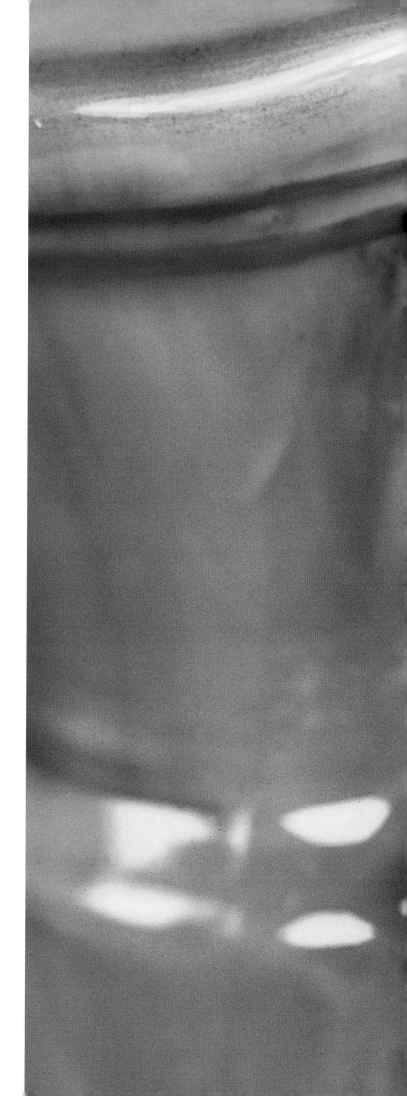

Conclusion

Today, pottery and faience from olden times are being taken out of attics, just as new ones are being created by potters who are in ever-greater demand. This is a fine history for these *objets d'art* that have already made their way in life. Born in Provence, they have traveled to the ends of the earth, from Africa to the Antilles to Quebec, and sometimes even to the depths of the sea in shipwrecks rich with sets of bowls, piles of dishes, and jars of oil.

This revival of interest extends far beyond France; one merely needs to look at the success Provençal pottery and faience has seen with Americans, for proof. But elsewhere as well, people envy the French this art.

But it is incumbent upon the French to relearn it. Finds occur by chance, and not knowing quite what to do with them, we pile them up in museums. For laughs, someone made up a festival of stuffing and another, of soups. He even wrote for himself scholarly works on *tians*. And one would be wrong to deny oneself—it's a real treat when the cooking is done in clay.

When a grandmother, a potter, and a gourmand meet, it is a whole past history that is reborn. The story starts all over again, for the greatest glory and the greatest pleasure of an *aïoli* and a *daube*. And the potters know this.

Bernard Duplessy

Selected Glossary

Barbotine: liquefied clay used to glue decorative elements, handles, buttons, etc. It is also the name given to highly colored ceramic objects with decorations in relief.

Biscuit (Biscuit or Bisque): material obtained after the first firing of the clay and before the painted decoration has been applied. By extension, the term also designates an object made in the material.

Camaïeu (Monochrome): decoration in a single hue such as ocher, yellow, green, violet, etc.

Céramique (Ceramic): an object made of pottery, stoneware, faience, or porcelain.

Chantourné (Jagged): a dish or plate with a rounded, irregular edge.

Dent de loup (Wolf-toothed): a painted scalloped edge on dishes or plates.

Engobe (Slip): a coating that colors the pottery.

Faïence (Faience): name derived from the Italian city of Faenza where the technique originated. Since the seventeenth century, the term was used to indicate a porous, fragile ceramic, made of clay with a tin-based glazing and fired at approximately 1830°F (1000°C).

Faïence fine (Fine faience): also called *terre de pipe* or pipe clay. A mixture of clays, flint, lime, feldspar, and kaolin all covered in a lead-based enamel. It arrived in France from England toward the end of the eighteenth century. Less expensive, it gradually entered French production starting in 1830.

Grand feu (High temperature): firing clay coated in a tin-based enamel at a temperature of 1830°F (1000°C), which causes the enamel to penetrate and become faience.

Grotesque: a fantastic, caricatural figure.

Magot: a grotesque from China, with a large head.

Oule (Olla): a clay stew pot.

Pégau: a gray, potbellied pot with one handle and a pouring spout. When the firing is done, the potter saturates it in carbon to make it waterproof.

Petit feu (Low temperature): firing done at around 1290° F (700° C) for faience with decorations added on already fired enamel. On the bottom, six marks from the *pernette* (a triangular support used during firings) can be seen. Firings at *grand feu* are never more than three.

Pignate: a clay stew pot thrown in the reverse (region of Vallauris).

Pissadou or Béringuière: a chamber pot.

Potager (Cooker): a kitchen furnishing that includes a brazier for slow cooking dishes such as stews or *daubes*.

Pot à oille: a circular pot with a lid for stews. It differs from the oval terrine, which holds meats and preceded the soup tureen, which would appear in the eighteenth century.

Poterie (Pottery): clay fired at high temperatures, often painted red (iron oxide), yellow (antimony oxide), green (copper oxide), and blue (cobalt oxide).

Safre (Zaffer): very fine sand composed of more than 90 percent silica.

Sartan: a frying pan.

Stannifière (Stannous): lead- and tin-based substance that creates a shiny white glazing; the tin content gives different nuances to the white.

Surtout (Centerpiece): centerpiece used for spices.

Taraïette: miniature replica of pottery; used as toys.

Taraille: terra-cotta dishware.

Tarasque: a fire damper in a half-bell shape, with handle.

Tian: a terra-cotta bowl or gratin plate.

Tomette: hexagonal floor tile.

Toupin: a clay pot with a handle and a pouring spout for heating liquids.

Toutouro: a varnished terra-cotta Saint-Jean trumpet that flares up over itself.

Viro-troucho: also *vire-omelette*. A platter for flipping an omelet.

Bibliography

Amouric, Henri, Florence Richez, and Lucy Vallauri. *Vingt mille pots sous les mers*. Musée d'Istres. Édisud, 1999.

———. *Des Ateliers et des hommes: Être céramiste à Aubagne aux XIXe et XXe siècles*. Exhibition catalogue. Thérèse Neveu, 2001.

Bats, Michel. "*Vaisselle et Alimentation à Olbia de Provence (c. 350–c. 50 BC)*" in *Revue Archéologique de Narbonnaise* (sup. 18). Éditions du CNRS, 1988.

Bertrand, Paul. *Faïences et Faïenciers de Varages*. Association Les Faïenciers de Varages, 83670 Varages, 1983.

Dumas, Marc. *Les Faïenciers d'Apt et du Castellet*. Édisud, 1990.

Études de céramiques à Aubagne et en Provence du XVIe au XXe siècle. Argilla 1991, Aubagne.

Les Faïences de La Tour-d'Aigues. Musée des Faïences, La Tour-d'Aigues, 1992.

Favelac, P. M. *Poteries rustiques*. Ch. Massin, undated.

Un Goût d'Italie: Céramiques et céramistes italiens en Provence du Moyen Âge au XXe siècle. Éditions Narration, Argilla 1993, Aubagne.

Julien, Louis. *L'Art de la faïence à Moustiers*. Édisud, 1991.

Lombard, Chantal. *Les Taraïettes provençales*. P. Tacussel Éditeur, 1987.

Mompeut, Jacques. *Les Faïences de Moustiers*. Édisud, 1980.

Pignates et poêlons: Poterie culinaire de Vallauris. Musée de la Céramique, Vallauris, 1996.

Raffaëli, Jeanne and Antoine. *La Faïencerie de Saint-Jean-du-Désert*. Maeght Éditeur, 1998.

Terres de Durance. Musée de Digne, Musée Départemental de Gap, 1995.

Terres de mémoire: 100 ans de céramique à Aubagne, XIXe–XXe siècles. Éditions Narration, Argilla 1995, Aubagne.

Ulisse, Nicole. *Salernes terre et céramique*. Édisud, 1987.

Useful Addresses

MUSEUMS

Musée Archéologique d'Apt
27, rue de l'Amphithéâtre
84400 Apt
Tel. +33 (0)4 90 74 78 45
Hours: Every day except Sunday (October to May)
and Tuesdays from 10am to noon and 2pm to 5:30pm.

Musée Archéologique de Pélissanne
Ancien Hôtel de Ville
Place Cabardel
13330 Pélissanne
Tel. +33 (0)4 90 55 11 87
Hours: Sundays from 10:30am to 12:30pm and by
appointment.

Museon Arlaten
29, rue de la République
13200 Arles
Tel. +33 (0)4 90 93 58 11
Hours: October through March, every day except
Monday from 9:30am to 12:30pm and 2pm to 5pm.
April to September, every day from 9:30am to
12:30pm and 2pm to 6pm.

Musée d'Art et d'Histoire de Provence
2, rue Mirabeau
06130 Grasse
Tel. +33 (0)4 93 36 01 61
Hours: October to May, every day except Tuesday
from 10am to 12:30pm and 2pm to 5:30pm. June to
September, every day from 10am to noon and 2pm
to 7pm.

**Musée des Arts et Traditions Populaires de
Draguignan**
Rue Joseph-Roumanille
83300 Draguignan
Tel. +33 (0)4 94 47 05 72

**Musée des Arts et Traditions Populaires du
Terroir Marseillais**
Château-Gombert
5, place des Héros
13013 Marseille
Tel. +33 (0)4 91 68 14 38

Musée de Draguignan
Rue de la République
83300 Draguignan
Tel. +33 (0)4 98 10 26 85

**Musée de la Faïence—Château Pastré Parc
Montredon**
155, avenue de Montredon
13008 Marseille
Tel. +33 (0)4 91 72 43 47
Hours: October to May, every day except Monday
from 10am to 5pm.

Musée des Faïences
Château de La Tour-d'Aigues
BP 48
84240 La Tour-d'Aigues
Tel. +33 (0)4 90 07 50 53
Hours: Monday to Friday from 9:30am to noon and
2pm to 6pm. Saturday and Sunday from 2pm to 6pm.

Musée des Faïences de Varages
Maison Gassendi
14, place de la Libération
83670 Varages
Tel. +33 (0)4 94 77 60 39
Hours: July through August, every day except
Monday from 10am to noon and 3pm to 7:30pm.
Off-season, every day except Monday and Tuesday
from 2pm to 6pm.

Musée d'Histoire Locale de Biot
6, place de la Chapelle
06410 Biot
Tel. +33 (0)4 93 65 54 54
Hours: Summer, every day except Monday and
Tuesday from 10am to 6pm. Off-season, every day
except Monday and Tuesday from 2pm to 6pm.

Musée d'Histoire de Marseille
Centre de la Bourse
13001 Marseille
Tel. +33 (0)4 91 90 42 22
Hours: Every day except Sunday from noon to 7pm.

Musée d'Histoire des Poteries
Association "Les Amis de la Poterie"
26270 Cliousclat
Tel. +33 (0)4 75 63 15 60 (museum)
Tel. +33 (0)4 75 63 22 42 (association)

Musée de Moustiers
Place du Tricentenaire
04360 Moustiers-Sainte-Marie
Tel. +33 (0)4 92 74 61 64
Hours: Every day except Tuesday from 9am to noon
and 2pm to 6pm.

Musée du Pays Brignolais—Palais des Comtes de Provence
Place des Comtes de Provence
83170 Brignoles
Tel. +33 (0)4 94 69 45 18
Hours: Summer, every day except Monday and
Tuesday from 9am to noon and 2:30pm to 6pm.
Off-season, every day except Monday and Tuesday
from 10am to noon and 2:30pm to 5pm.

Musée du Petit Palais
21, place du Petit Palais
84000 Avignon
Tel. +33 (0)4 90 86 44 58

Musée de la Poterie
Rue Sicard
06220 Vallauris
Tel. +33 (0)4 93 64 66 51
Hours: Summer, from 10:30am to 7pm. Off-season,
from 10:30am to 5:30pm.

Musée de la Préhistoire des Gorges du Verdon
Route de Montmeyan
04500 Quinson
Tel. +33 (0)4 92 74 09 59

POTTERY MAKERS AND
FAÏENCERIES

L'Arrosoir
5, rue Justin-Jouve
26220 Dieulefit
Tel. +33 (0)4 75 90 60 83

Atelier Bernard—Jean Faucon
286, avenue de la Libération
84400 Apt
Tel. +33 (0)4 90 74 15 31

Atelier du Soleil
Chemin de Quinson
04360 Moustiers-Sainte-Marie
Tel. +33 (0)4 92 74 63 05

Barbotine—Philippe Beltrando
Rue Paul-Ruer
13400 Aubagne
Tel. +33 (0)4 42 70 03 00

Poterie Pierre Basset
Quartier des Arnauds
83690 Salernes
Tel. +33 (0)4 94 70 70 70

Faïencerie de la Belle Époque
2, rue de la Paix
83670 Varages
Tel. +33 (0)4 94 77 64 95

Faïencerie Bondil
Place de l'Église
Boîte Postale 5
04360 Moustiers-Sainte-Marie
Tel. +33 (0)4 92 74 67 02

Poterie Calicot—Odile Cazanave-Pin
Le Village
26270 Mirmande
Tel. +33 (0)4 75 63 21 86

Poterie de Cliousclat
Le Village
26270 Cliousclat
Tel. +33 (0)4 75 63 05 69

Atelier Jean-Michel Coquet
Quartier Les Jas
13116 Vernègues
Tel. +33 (0)4 90 59 30 85
Hours: Every day except Sunday from 9am to noon
and 2pm to 7pm.

Poterie Éric Desplanches
Place de l'Église
13105 Mimet
Tel. +33 (0)4 42 58 93 85

Faïencerie Figuères
10-12, avenue Lauzier
13008 Marseille
Tel. +33 (0)4 91 73 06 79

Poterie Corinne et Philippe Gauthier
Ancien Moulin à Huile (Old Oil Mill)
Rue des Moulins
83570 Montfort-sur-Argens
Tel. +33 (0)4 94 59 52 19

Poterie "Il était une fois"
Place de l'Ancien Collège
26220 Dieulefit
Tel. +33 (0)4 75 46 87 58

Poterie Massucco
Villa Claude
Camp Major
13400 Aubagne
Tel. +33 (0)4 42 03 34 31

La Poterie Provençale—Augé-Laribé
1689, route de la Mer
06410 Biot
Tel. +33 (0)4 93 65 63 30

Poterie Ravel
Avenue des Goums
13400 Aubagne
Tel. +33 (0)4 42 18 79 79

Dominique Reboul—Antiquités: Poteries et Art Populaire
Galerie "Le Quai de la Gare"
4, avenue Julien-Guigue
84800 L'Isle-sur-la-Sorgue
Tel. +33 (0)4 66 80 22 18 and (0)6 07 46 27 07
Hours: Saturday, Sunday, and Monday from 10am to 7pm.

Poterie Jean Robin
Quartier de la Rivière
26160 Le Poët-Laval
Tel. +33 (0)4 75 46 48 40

Poterie Saltalamacchia
48, avenue Georges-Clemenceau
06220 Vallauris
Tel. +33 (0)4 93 64 67 20

Santons Fouque
65, cours Gambetta
13100 Aix-en-Provence
Tel. +33 (0)4 42 26 33 38
Hours: Every day except Sunday and holidays, from 9am to noon and 2pm to 6pm.

Poterie Cathy et Gilles Sias
Le Village
84110 Séguret
Tel. +33 (0)4 90 46 97 20

Tamba Poteries—Le Four à Chaud
Route de Malaucène
84330 Caromb
Tel. +33 (0)4 90 62 41 87

Les Terres Cuites—Sismondini
Route de Sillans—La Cascade
83690 Salernes
Tel. +33 (0)6 09 07 67 28

Perrine Thoumyre—Restauration de Céramiques
Route des Carrières
84580 Oppède
Tel. +33 (0)4 90 76 95 06 and (0)6 07 64 51 32

Vernin—Le Carreau d'Apt
Route Nationale 100
Pont Julien
84480 Bonnieux
Tel. +33 (0)4 90 04 63 04
Hours: From 9am to noon and 2pm to 6pm

List of Illustrations

Acknowledgments

I would like to thank all those who helped to make this book around the largest *tian* in the world. But it would be meters wide in circumference and there exists no kiln large enough for firing.

Thus, all that remains is to give my thanks, in these few lines, to the museum staffs, the pottery staffs, and the potters themselves who appear in these pages and who, with their warm wishes, gave permission for the use of their photographs. And also to these women who cook in clay: Madame Mas, Dromel de Monieux, and Rosette de Mimet, champion of ravioli. And dame Pognate. They have entrusted me with their secrets.

All photographs used in this work are by Camille Moirenc, with the exception of:
Collection Roger-Viollet: pages 17 and 33; Collection Kharbine-Tapabor: pages
30 and 32.

Project Manager, English-language edition: Susan Richmond
Editor, English-language edition: David J. Baker
Jacket design, English-language edition: Michael Walsh and Brankica Kovrlija
Design Coordinator, English-language edition: Tina Thompson

Library of Congress Cataloging-in-Publication Data
Duplessy, Bernard.
  The French country table : pottery and faience of Provence / text by
Bernard Duplessy ; photographs by Camille Moirenc ; translated from the
French by Laurel Hirsch.
p. cm.
Includes bibliographical references.
ISBN 0-8109-4578-9
1. Pottery craft—France—Provence. 2. Faience—France—Provence.
3. Pottery—History. 4. Kitchen utensils—France—Provence. I. Title.

TT919.7.F8P76 2003
738'.0944'9—dc21

2003000328

Printed and bound in Spain
10 9 8 7 6 5 4 3 2 1

Harry N. Abrams, Inc.
100 Fifth Avenue
New York, N.Y. 10011
www.abramsbooks.com

Abrams is a subsidiary of